REFLECTIONS

REFLECTIONS

An Anthology of New Work by African Women Poets

edited by
Anthonia C. Kalu
Juliana Makuchi Nfah-Abbenyi
Omofolabo Ajayi-Soyinka

LYNNE
RIENNER
PUBLISHERS

BOULDER
LONDON

Published in the United States of America in 2013 by
Lynne Rienner Publishers, Inc.
1800 30th Street, Boulder, Colorado 80301
www.rienner.com

and in the United Kingdom by
Lynne Rienner Publishers, Inc.
3 Henrietta Street, Covent Garden, London WC2E 8LU

Library of Congress Cataloging-in-Publication Data
Kalu, Anthonia C.
  Reflections : an anthology of new work by African women poets /
edited by Anthonia C. Kalu, Juliana Makuchi Nfah-Abbenyi, and
Omofolabo Ajayi-Soyinka.
     p.   cm.
  Includes index.
  ISBN 978-1-58826-868-6 (alk. paper)
  1. African poetry—Women authors. 2. African poetry—21st century.
3. American poetry—African American authors. 4. American poetry
—Women authors. 5. American poetry—21st century.
  I. Kalu, Anthonia C. II. Nfah-Abbenyi, Juliana Makuchi, 1958–
III. Ajayi-Soyinka, Omofolabo.
  PL8013.E5R44 2013
  808.810082—dc23

                                                    2012041548

British Cataloguing in Publication Data
A Cataloguing in Publication record for this book
is available from the British Library.

Printed and bound in the United States of America

The paper used in this publication meets the requirements
of the American National Standard for Permanence of
Paper for Printed Library Materials Z39.48-1992.

5 4 3 2 1

Contents

Kenya

Introduction

Anthonia C. Kalu,
Juliana Makuchi Nfah-Abbenyi,
and Omofolabo Ajayi-Soyinka

Although a number of African women writers have made their presence felt in prose fiction and drama, the voices of women poets are relatively in short supply on the contemporary African literary scene. This anthology of previously unpublished poems by African women is a tribute to their enduring creativity and an acknowledgment of their individual and collective efforts to enrich African literature. Their poems reflect the diversity of African women's experiences, observations, and thinking about a wide range of issues on the continent and globally—love, identity, family, politics, sexuality, motherhood, hunger, hope, war, peace, and more. The poets' new perspectives propel readers to a contemporary Africa and beyond popular stereotypes of African womanhood. The subjects addressed in this collection are accessible and of broad interest.

A brief examination of these poems confirms Africa's violent social and political transitions as questions of individual and national identity are challenged daily. The poems showcase the nature and pervasiveness of the current cultures of violence while revealing the extent to which Africa and Africans are struggling to maintain normality. This view of normality does not ignore precolonial violence or suffering; rather, it highlights indigenous social norms that existed before European incursions in Africa.

African poetry, one of the continent's most fully developed

verbal art traditions (there are poems for every occasion and for every age), features a variety of forms and styles arising from the varied nature of life and experience on the continent. Thus, one cannot speak of a representative African poetic tradition. However, although there are great variations in poetic form, style, and theme, it is possible to recognize shared features in poems from various parts of the continent. These features arise from an unstated but commonly known core of African principles and experiences. Most of the traditions that characterize the poetic styles are transmitted by women who keep both content and form current by passing on knowledge and practices to subsequent generations.

Praise poems, like many other types, vary in focus, style, and delivery from group to group. Often recited, these poems speak of ordinary individuals, warriors, family and friends, and even about cattle and other possessions. Contemporary African women poets also use praise poetry to explore political, historical, and social life, as well as women's status in the family, society, and the nation. Some works acknowledge the trials of being wives, mothers, and sisters. Susan Kiguli's "Guilty," for example, portrays the African woman as an enduring and loving mother. Other contemporary praise poets celebrate African women's physical beauty and their self-determined leadership roles in the continent's history. Lydia E. Epangué's "Mamazon," an accolade to the physical and symbolic beauty of African womanhood, concludes:

> And when she finally hands over that baton,
> Mamazon will soar like a star to watch over me.
> And it is not a gravestone I shall place over her head.
> It shall be a Crown.

Toyin Adewale-Gabriel, in "Sister Cry," asserts the bonds of African women leaders across generations and issues a strident call for rethinking decades of the "herstory" of successful Nigerian women leaders. In addition to incorporating the Western feminist concept of sisterhood into the thinking of educated contemporary African women, Adewale-Gabriel also appropriates traditional praise poetry's exhortative role in times of war and calls attention to African women's leadership in local and national arenas. Summoning African women to action, "Sister Cry" begins:

> We are women of the corn rows plaits,
> Wrapper rooted, song strong, waists fastened with
>   determined cloth.
> We are herstory, our stories sit in our wombs.

These contemporary praise poets have found ways to advance this traditional poetic form while engaging in discussions about African women's efforts to assert their rights and to defend their ability to be active as local and national leaders without neglecting their responsibilities as mothers and teachers.

African children are introduced to poetry through lullabies, chants, and songs that are embedded in folktales to encourage retention of content and meaning. Some children's chants and songs are used to settle minor disputes and to accompany various events, including rites of passage. As children age, praise poems are introduced to enable and propel individual identity and identification within the group. Several poems in this collection are used in this manner as the poets continue efforts to rebuild, revise, and maintain childhood memories about Africa's paths to independence, including the dilemma of maintaining African identities in the long postindependence battle over the use of African and European languages. Some of the poems retain rhythms and cadences of traditional forms and styles; others speak across growing social and political divides, remembering, bridging, and healing differences while looking for ways to tell new stories that reveal new truths to today's children. Still others tell stories that are old and unforgettable, but unspeakable: stories of incest, rape, and female genital surgeries and the use of children as soldiers and prostitutes. Those growing up in Africa today have much to fear, as seen in Oghomwen Adeyinka-Edward's "The Fear of Broken Dishes"; however, as Adewale-Gabriel advocates in "Sister Cry," African women should continue to write poems that confront transformative change and to participate in the discussion by "asking for what we must give, a sacrifice of gold / a basket of courage, a strident voice."

Although poetry continues to influence and shape a significant part of creativity in African verbal arts, it is one of the major casualties of colonization as is evidenced in contemporary African literature's debates about the language question. During the colonial period, the need for expertise in the colonizers' languages restrained indigenous self-expression as Africa's schoolchildren learned poems in European languages in Western-style classrooms. However, this volume shows that contemporary African artists did not lose the ability to harness aspects of cultural memory from indigenous languages. It is interesting to note the extent to which some of the poets in this book refuse to shun African verse and its rich layered meanings and have worked Africa's diverse language vistas into their poems by basing their work on the premise that all languages that have touched Africa's homeland and cultures are part of contemporary Africa, its experiences and expressions. Their approach is different from early Western-style educational and discursive strategies in Africa that perceived indigenous languages and indigenous poetic traditions as irrelevant. This contemporary approach is seen in Lamia Zayzafoon's "Milk of the Ogre" and Harriet Naboro's blending of five languages in "Leave Me Alone." Thus, some contributors strive for new rhythms that incorporate Africa's cultural experiences and values into the postindependence environment.

While influenced by indigenous poetic forms, the postindependence poetry of many African women reflects deep familiarity with Western feminism and feminist thinking. Some poems also explore African womanism (an alternative to Western feminism) and other analytical approaches to women's issues and experiences. Social criticism is central to their works; a prevailing theme is giving women's voices to Africa's current dilemmas. Part of the struggle includes the refusal of contemporary African women to adhere to views of African women held by Western feminists. Thérèse Kuoh-Moukoury's "The Lost Throne" implicitly rejects the idea of the African woman as a beast of burden, always carrying heavy loads, by celebrating different parts of the African mother's body as a seat of power for her children. Seen from the point of view of the emotionally healthy child nurtured and shielded by the African mother's body, Kuoh-Moukoury's poem acknowledges the African woman as both a responsible and a joyful mother. Sarah Navalayo Osembo's "When Daddy Had an Affair" points to the far-reaching consequences of infidelity as it details the pain children experience when they have to deal on their own with knowledge of the secrets of adults' untidy, complex lives. Temitope Azeez-Stephen's "Funeral Theme" and Arecau's "You, and Your Four Loved Ones" keep discussions about relations between African women and men open to further appraisal and negotiation. It is encouraging to note the ways that several contributors address the question of romantic love. Refuting the assumption that romantic love is foreign to relationships between African men and women, some poems, like Edna Merey Apinda's "The Secret of the Night," are lyrical and sweet, while "Funeral Theme" roils with the unalloyed anger and frustrations of a relationship that has come to an end.

A brief look at the study of the oral tradition in Africa shows that practitioners and scholars tend to agree on the African woman's role as storyteller. She is perceived as one who straddles traditions and creates a bridge between generations. As a result, her responsibility to make sense of contemporary Africa accrues as the continent struggles with development that is stunted by violence in all areas of life. Although African women's roles as competent performers of the oral narrative are evident in the depictions of some female characters in contemporary African fiction, discussions of the creative potential of female poets remain scanty. Compared to material in the oral tradition, the dearth of published poems by contemporary African women might suggest either the absence of poetic vision in the oral narrative tradition of which women are said to be expert practitioners or the absence of African women's creativity in this area of traditional and contemporary African verbal arts. This collection's presentation of new works by seventy-one African women poets demonstrates that African women's interest in this aspect of Africa's verbal arts is vibrant. While they address enduring topics such as colonialism, negritude, corruption, and failed leadership, they also introduce new subjects of interest to readers. Some poems address infidelity, divorce, female genital surgeries, and HIV/AIDS, which until recently many African women preferred to address only in private.

Several poems in this anthology continue the discussion about the need to educate women, as well as the consequences that educated women face. Some of the poems also show how these new writers' skills are changing to accommodate Africa's engagement with important ideas and issues in the global marketplace. The poems as a whole illustrate the diversity in language, technology, and other bases of knowledge that are quickly becoming part of the lives of Africans worldwide.

Reflections complements Stella and Frank Chipasula's *The Heinemann Book of African Women's Poetry* (1995); Tanure Ojaide and Tijan Sallah's *The New African Poetry* (2000), a collection of poems by both women and men; and Irene D'Almeida and Janis Mayes's *A Rain of Words: A Bilingual Anthology of Women's Poetry in Francophone Africa* (2009). The poets whose works appear in this anthology are from Botswana, Burkina Faso, Cameroon, Egypt, Gabon, Ghana, Kenya, Namibia, Nigeria, Rwanda, South Africa, Tanzania, Tunisia, Uganda, Zambia, and Zimbabwe. Immediately apparent is the large number of contributions from Nigeria—understandable because in the history of African literature to date and for a reason that is yet to be understood, Nigerian writers seem to be enjoying a season of abundant creativity. The second largest group of contributors is from Kenya. Next, we acknowledge the versatile participation of the Uganda Women Writers' Association (FEMRITE), whose promotion of African women's collaboration through writing and publication is worthy of emulation.

Many of the contributors to the volume are well-known poets and writers. Their subjects speak to the issues that Africans face daily and to the efforts they make to confront and resolve them. The poets are from all walks of life, and their works point to a clearly developed self-awareness of contemporary African women's writing. *Reflections* corroborates the extent to which African women are paying attention to global issues and subsequent dynamics that affect their lives, roles, functions, and participation. It is difficult to ignore the prevailing sense of loss expressed in many of the poems in this anthology—even in the poems that deal primarily with love, understanding, and progress. Nevertheless, whatever their focus, the poems assert the fact that African women continue to pool their resources as they work to subvert power and deny authority to both traditional and modern efforts aimed at silencing women and according them second-class citizenship on the continent and abroad. The assertion of self-worth is a pervasive theme in these poems, but what is instructive is the extent to which the contemporary African woman poet speaks out for positive change worldwide.

NORTH AFRICA

Egypt
Tunisia

EGYPT

Nadia Z. Bishai

Stardust

stardust
is all it takes
to make a universe
and new people
who can hate
and perhaps love
a tired breed bending
under the burden
of many desert moons

Blazing in Deserts

blazing in deserts
the winds
whistle words
whose letters are made
of sand
rattling
then jumbling the truth
with no one to say
what order they should come in

Lamia Ben Youssef Zayzafoon

Milk of the Ogre
(In Memory of My Father)

أعذروه اللّي تكوى بفراق غزاله

مشى حبيب قلبه وأشتاق خياله

ما بقى له والو

لا شي يحلى له

يا ربي ماله؟

Mercy on him who by the ghazal's departure doth burn!
The bygone's shadow he now misses.
God! What is to become of him
He who no sweetness has left anymore?
                                        —Emile Zrihan

My body is in the North, my soul is in the South.
Who better sings my loss
Than a Maghribi Jew who moves East to mourn his West?
Your voice in vain I searched
Chez Victor,
At the place de la monnaie,
At the BNA,*
And at Harissa.com.
"I haven't had a good meal since the Jews left Tunisia!"
You used to say.
I went online looking for the *freshk, metthawma* and *bqaila* recipes
To be home with you!
I baked your lost paradise, but to my table you did not come.

---

* La Banque Nationale Agricole, where her father used to work.

Then, I wore your green shirt and went looking for the
    ogress's milk—
Walking in your footsteps,
Sipping your words,
And gobbling your kosher *kaakmadeleines*.

* * *

In an all men Turkish bath, a four-year old Moorish girl twirls
    and sings under the light of
Her father's eye. A woman screams her husband has gone crazy!
    He must be put in chains.

On the eve of the Yom Kippur War, a first grader, hit by a car,
    is taken by strangers to
Breathe in her father's smoke-filled *Caisse Locale.*
Under the *taqaseem* of her father's typewriter, the rescued girl is
    playing with pens,
Papers, strings, and staples under the red *kabbous,*[†] warm eyes,
    toothless mouth and black
        hands of 'Am Khmayes.
At the Thuburbo Majus, two school-girls, in dismay, contemplate
    the shells of
Unwelcome *oeufs de vin* on the stairs of their Father's House.

On the carpets of red poppies and daffodils lying beyond the
    railway bridge, a girl rides
For the first time a blue bike under the loving sun of her
    father and Si 'Amor.

At the Belvédère, a little girl in front of the North Pole white bear
    swallows her gum and
Clings closer to the rims of her father's coat.

---

† *Kabbous* is a traditional Tunisian wool hat usually worn by men.

In the hot Tunis-Pont du Fahs Louage of 'Am Fredj, rises the
    heavenly *odœmétissage* of
Belgian chocolates, *fricassés,* kaki and pralines that Father Ma'zuziya[$]
    brings his hungry
        Kids at nightfall.

In the long summer siestas at Le Kram, a dozen children gather to
    hear the picaresque
Adventures of Larget from Buk El Hich, the indefatigable and
    intarissable neighborhood
        Storyteller-irrigator.

At Mateur, every Friday night a father brings his daughter the
    cave of Ali Baba bedecked
With Pif & Hercule, Blec Le Roc, Fantômas, Zembla, Tintin,
    and the Janus-like Rex.

At Ben Arous, a father recites to his daughters the rainbow verses of
    the moon: from the
Jahiliyan stories of Imru 'ul Qais and Baraqish, who caused her own
    demise, to the
Umayyad poet al Hutay'a, who finding no one else to satirize,
    stung himself with the
        Venom of his own tongue.

At Rue Abou Kacem Chebbi, every night a father tacks his
    daughters into bed singing des
        Lamiabinties and Hajlabinties.

At Djebel Jeloud #22 bus stop, a father pours buttermilk over
    the head of a young man
Who dared to flirt-knock on Scheherazade's window.

[$] The reference is to the North African version of "The Wolf and the Seven Young Kids."
Tunisian sociologist Abdelwaheb Bouhdiba studies this folktale in *L'imaginaire Maghrebin:
Étude de dix contes pour enfants* (Tunis: M.T.E., 1977).

At Year of the Baccalaureate, a father travels to Vaga every weekend
to shower his
Daughter with books, love, pistachios and *intitrigelwananrigels*!

In Hadrumete, a father knocks on his daughter's dorm with
his foot, because his hands
Are too loaded with *frishk* and *harsa* from Chez Victor, cakes
and pâtés from La
Parisienne, Pizza from El Memmi, soap, and cheese and
tuna cans from Le Magasin
Général.

At the *Banque Nationale Agricole*, a father, in front of his friends,
teases his daughter
Who came to pick up her weekly allowance: "Look at her! Eh!
All of this lipstick and no
Boyfriend!"

In Michigan, a thirty-two year graduate student seeks the
amniotic in Kristeva's chora
And severs her umbilical cord with her Oriental father.
In the spring that arose from the Y2K hysteria, a soon to be
evil-doer who devours his
Children sends his life savings to pay for the surgery of his
"First World" one-month
Grandson.

In Dixie Land, the triply orphaned daughter gouges her eyes out:
If only she tried harder to belong!
If only she could repaint her father's home with the beaming
thunder of his voice! If only
She could smell the *neffa* and red and purple daffodils in her
father's garden! If only she
Could see his smile on the iris of the moon!

* * *

On the first anniversary of your departure,
I sang on I-65 S "The Bygone's Shadow I now Miss!"
This time you heard my umbilical call.
That same night,
You returned to say goodbye.
With no visa,
And undetected by Homeland Security Eye
You sneaked from the *fronteras* of the beyond,
Wearing your Calvin Klein black suit
And red tie:
You always loved pranks!
You were walking laughing and teasing your tormentor:
"Thy eye shall close like mine! Thy eye shall close like mine!"
For a brief moment, the curtain was lifted,
And I swam once more in the ogre's river of milk and honey.
Then your shade released its embrace and flew away,
Leaving me as only gift,
The joy of sorrow!

The Beautiful Widow of the Green Mountain

The Beautiful Widow of the Green Mountain
"*Bessalamah** ā 'Allala!
Why did you leave me behind? "
Screamed she in a bittersweet pain,
At the coffin of her companion,
Of thirty-six years,
At present,
A seventy-three pound mass of bones,
Carried by sons and male relatives to The Last Home!
Yesterday,
He was released
From the jaws of
Doctors,
Clinics,
X-Rays,
Cat scans,
The smell of labs,
And the shame
Of not dying in dignity:
Of having to reveal,
At the dusk of one's life,
What ought to remain hidden.

* * *

In that cruel April afternoon,
In an upscale hill of Vaga,
People stood in awe—
Puzzled by
The strange beauty
Of the widow,
Who appeared
On the terrace
To salute

---

* *Bessalamah* means good-bye in Tunisian Arabic dialect.

The curious and envious eyes
Of those who came to offer their sympathy.
No woman has ever looked so beautiful,
Not even her on her wedding day.
It is the beauty of a woman
Whose hair turned gray overnight!
Her eyes, deaf
As an ocean with no waves!
And her ears, blind
As a sky with no birds!

* * *

Twenty five days earlier, 'Allala told his wife:
"Buy the *jebbas* that you liked the other day.
Don't worry about the price!
I want you to look your best, always,
Even on and after the Day of my Exit."
It was in this final present
That Nabiha dressed up to say farewell to her beloved husband.

* * *

"Now that you have become bald,
You have to observe the *'udda*,"
Rose in chorus,
The voice of Nabiha's mother Lalla Fattouma,
And the twelve policing eyes
Of Si 'Allala's sisters.
"Take off this jebba! My brother was a lion, not a cat,"
    said one of the sisters.
"How can she take a shower, wear a new *jebba*, and wear
    a deodorant on his funeral?"
The *hajala*† of the Green Mountain
Must now be deprived
Of the joys of wifehood:

---

† *Hajala* means widow in Arabic dialect.

No sugar-wax,
No tweezers,
No hairdresser,
No new clothes,
No kohl,
No lipstick.
No perfume.
No weddings.
No circumcision ceremonies.
No TV.
No music.
No vacations.
No flea market.
Poor Nabiha!
Bewailed all the women at the funeral
Your house is empty!
And your head is naked!
Your time is over. *Wfa!*
Tout est fini! The end!

Postscript note: Twenty five days after the death of her husband, Nabiha heard that the Columbian singer Shakira was on the list of international singers invited to Carthage International Festival. "'Udda or no 'udda," Nabiha said, "I will buy myself a blond wig and go to the concert incognito! My husband has always wanted me to have fun!" Shakira's concert turned out to be a rumor, unfortunately.

CENTRAL AND EAST AFRICA

Gabon
Kenya
Rwanda
Tanzania
Uganda

Jasmine Ntoutoume

Noises in the Blood

SHI GOT NOISES
IN THE BLOOD
it-a-bwayl, it-a-curdle
it-a-jump evri hurdle
DEFIANCE!
She arrived as a black bone doll,
a living corpse
Screamin', bleedin', packed too tight
scarred on body,
marked in mind
Only the fittest survived . . .

SHI *STILL* GOT NOISES
IN THE BLOOD
it-a-bwayl, it-a-curdle
it-a-jump evri hurdle
DEFIANCE!
She can dance, she can turn her sorrows
into her woman warrior dance
She'll take the chance to show
that
Rome-ate-Romance

She's a Sound-System-Salome *Go-Go*
She lifts it, hitches it, pitches it
She'll spread her wings to

fly away

An'when di pow*ah* not in balance
It mean di pow*ah* not shared
and when darkness turns to light
She'll catch the enemy running scared

SHI GOT NOISES
IN THE BLOOD
it-a-bwayl, it-a-curdle
it-a-jump *evri* hurdle
DEFIANCE!
She's a warrior gyal
Fightin' for di noises in 'ar blood
for the soul she's bold
Can't bank on beauty
An di-pen-a-lone can't win
it mus turn a tousand tongue tips into pointed spears
AHA !

SHI WILL ALWAYS HAVE NOISES
IN THE BLOOD
it-a-bwayl, it-a-curdle
it-a-jump e-ve-ry hurdle
DEFIANCE!

Edna Merey Apinda

The Secret of the Night

Tell the wind
To carry away these words
Towards the one for whom
My heart is beating

Tell the river
To carry my steps
Towards the one
Who waits for me

Tell time
To stop
When it fixes
Its gaze on me

Tell the night
To be very discrete
Keeping to itself alone
The secret of our lips

Tell the dawn
To delay coming
So that our hands may still
Remain interlaced

Translated from the French by Cheryl Toman. The original version of the poem appears
in the Appendix on page 169.

Little Does It Matter

I sing, I dance, I laugh
I live as if tomorrow does not exist
I lie as if no one was listening to me
Life sweeps me up like a soft melody
I move ahead without worrying about the future

But sometimes
When night falls and no one is listening
I say a secret prayer
So that tomorrow may be lucid
Full of promises

Since often
Life is sad on this side of the planet
It shows how it can be cruel
Leaving some orphaned, starving, or disturbed
As they run
Towards more riches by selling their souls to the devil
Forgetting he who lives high in the heavens

I sing, I dance
I laugh, I live
As if tomorrow will be sweeter
I dream that it will be more simple
Like days gone by

Since all too often
People move along like beasts of burden
Strung along by preachers of a different kind
Who look to the bottoms of pocketbooks
In order to lead souls to God

Translated from the French by Cheryl Toman. The original version of the poem appears in the Appendix on page 170.

We think we are fooling life
Life that makes us ugly or poor
We always want more out of it
And why ?
We fear tomorrow, the other, our fellow man
We believe ourselves superior to everything

But we are only human
And tomorrow
Will find us such as we are
Beggars on a quest for love
Believers hoping for salvation
The destitute with a heart of gold
Humans

I sing a tender melody
I mock the new false prophets, king in this country
I cry before the human being who is lost
In a quest for money at any cost
Values disappear and I hope
For a tomorrow that will be better
That will sing
That will make us dance

Imali J. Abala

Freedom Shall Be Ours

Freedom shall be ours!
Freedom shall be ours!
Bellowed the youth of a torn nation
Defenseless mercenaries of peace
Who bear the brunt of unemployment
Who bear the brunt of poverty
Who bear the brunt of hopelessness.
Step by step, they marched,
Like dutiful soldiers at a lieutenant's bark,
Thronging the ghostly streets of Nairobi—
      Empty, Dead, Broken—
Lured by sweet melodies of hope.
And like accursed simpletons,
They walked into a den of armed brutes!
Alas, the emerging conscience of a torn nation,
Tear gassed by demagogues of power,
Fell one-by-one.
Their broken limbs knew no pain!
Justice shall be ours! Justice shall be ours,
Heckled the youth of a torn nation!

Dimwitted and uniformed,
Demagogues of brute force,
Like actors in a theatre of the absurd,
Plugged their ears, muffling the cries of the fallen,
Closed their eyes to decapitated bodies of the fallen.
Alas, the conscience of a torn nation dead,
Yet, tomorrow,
When they ascend the freedom stairs,
The revolutionary mercenaries of justice,
Shall sing: Freedom is ours!

The Conundrum of My Life

I died long before I knew my name
      Long before I muttered my first syllable
      Long before I lost my first tooth
      Long before I was submerged in the Holy books
      Long before I shed my first blood
      Long before I lost my innocence
So, don't ask me why I am not myself
      I was indoctrinated to despise my tongue
      I was indoctrinated to hate my ebony skin
      I was indoctrinated to be ashamed of my short hair
      I was indoctrinated to loathe my unschooled mother
      I was indoctrinated to abhor my flesh and blood
Thus, I fell into the chasms of knowledge
      And like a bat in a daylight flight
      Fell into the *pure* and *unadulterated* Faith of the West
      Fell head over heels in love with my modern education
      Fell prey to the tight-jean mentality of my youth
      Fell into the mini-skirt traps of my adolescent life
      Fell into the romantic love traps of the West
      Never having learned a thing of substance of my culture
Therefore, don't cry for me
      For your tears will be wasted
      A dead woman is not worth a tear
      A dead existence is nothing to fret over
      I died long before I knew my name
      Long before I produced an heir
      Long before I was put six feet under
      For there, in the depth of earth,
      I shall forever remain
      Unknown
      Unacknowledged!

Arecau

A New Moon

Why do I blame the moon for this?
When it is you.

Imagine;
our worlds converging for a time.

Here
it feels we will remain entwined.

But our universe implodes;
And our worlds,
no longer in congress.

So I mourn the loss;
The loss of this full moon.

How can I see in all this darkness?

This is not a love poem,
You are not the seed of my life,
Let me assure you of that.

This is just a formal declaration
of my anger at letting you go.

A Minor Death

Give in to me and become weak to the touch of my hands.

Do anything for me.
Cry when I make you come

Please—
Wrap your hands so tightly around my neck that I feel
like I'm dying.

You, and Your Four Loved Ones

The room we rent;
Bare and blue.
Sparse and clean.

We become lovers quickly.
Your heavy bag lands upon
the softness of our lovemaking;
Suddenly I'm with you, and you with me and I call your name.

My name, you call over and over.
Until I have no more to give.
All you can give me, you pour out
onto the skin above my heart, my chin.

You know when you pull out of me, your eyes tighten?
It looks like weeping lays by your eyes—
Ready to inundate from a crevice
That I will never reach.

We keep in the shadows, we refuse to let go.
In stillness, I clutch to the up of your back,
your cradling arms imprison me.

We use conversation to reconstruct our crumbling world.
Weight bears down heavy on these feeble buttresses.
The army is closing in.
Our world, our words,
are scribbled, revised, re-visioned.

Between our sexing
I visit the loo; its hungry hole rests beneath me.
The bathroom door is closed, I run the tap,
I'm embarrassed you'll hear the sound of my relief.
I wash my sex of my stickiness,
I wipe you off my stomach.

My yearning becomes larger than these four walls;
this frosted window.
Apart on weeknights, I rub easy and fast,
Imitating that deep down pushing, imagining—
our moving bodies under streamed light,
a bathroom door left ajar.

Sometimes you push so hard,
I'm sore for days, I itch, push tablets into my hollowness.

Then you discard of what you no longer want, pack what you need.
You tell me to dress
"I have responsibilities, you know?
No contact!
Send me a postcard if you have to—
keep the greeting platonic."

In your absence I write a letter.
My words;
illustrations.
Allow me to draw a large lady—

Your wide, flat-tipped fingers tight at her throat, rendering
    her breathless.
Submission rounds the slits of her eyes,
You stare at your reflection, erratic, thrusts, pushing,
    hungrily into her.
She begs, you take.
I envelop it,
I attach an arbitrary photograph of a couple; cameras in
    their respective hands, in an
outlandish place, they immortalize some gorgeous,
    god forsaken land.

I receive no reply.
I venture to see you. I find you in an armchair;
your children's tender hands wrapped around your neck,
your beard, wet with their gentle kisses.
You don't see me.
You watch your wife; she is perfect, ideally breasted, firm,
    ever loving.
Tonight's dinner is almost ready.

Bonita Belle

God Helps Those Who Help Themselves

I can't save everyone

Heck I can't even save myself!
all these years, still the same old drama
all these tears still the constant trauma
of being afraid to let go

to get up
to shut up
to sleep

I can't care about everyone
Yet those who need me the most I neglect
those that hurt me I am constantly their reject
always their second choice
and yet nothing compares to me
no one really intimidates me
I can do all things if I put my mind to it
Yet here I am
here we are

still asking God to save us
still reciting Invictus
and waking up with the same headache
finding it hard to save your joy
letting passerbys steal it
will it
ever end?

I love you
but I can't save you
not anymore

Rose Wanjiru Busolo

Sometimes I Wonder

Sometimes I wonder
about the way things are
about the way I wish they were
and about all I wish they weren't
for I sure know what I want

Sometimes I wonder
why it seems so hard
why it's always so much harder
to sit and wish I hadn't
taken the time to care

Sometimes I wonder
who it will ever be
whoever it may even be
waiting at the wings
at the end of the dark tunnel

Sometimes I wonder
If I know the way
If I really have the sway
that all time cure
that's sure as the day

Sometimes I wonder
about all the doors I knock
about all the times I've knocked

Anastacia Kamau

Mmh! People

A silent wail echoes across the ridges,
and in hushed tones word is spread
in so many distorted versions,
each new version more wicked than the last,
some said AIDS, others TB
others SUICIDE, yet others a CURSE

So they all came,
some to confirm that he was really expired,
and others to know the cause of his expiration,
some were genuine while others were fake,
so they all gathered and wept,
t'was gloom, t'was expected,

"From dust to dust, ashes to ashes" the priest said,
from the oldest to the youngest each put a handful of soil,
with tears, grief, pain and much wailing,
they bid him farewell,
with dejected footsteps they filed away,
but not before they had their stomachs fill,

Those that truly loved him agonized,
as they heard the hushed rumours,
those that loved him were dismayed,
as they watched them go,
all in a traditional farewell,
but what to do my friend?

Njeri Kang'ethe

Between My Legs

A surprise, a, special gift was I;
A bonus to parents long past child bearing age;
But one look at the spot between my legs;
And my fate was sealed.
My mother looked away in shame;
My father's faked bravado
could not hide his bitter disappointment;
Silence pregnant with despair;
for who would dare speak when the sun turns his face?
Darkness at noon, a blot in a house
that boasted nothing less than the birth of sons.

What shall we call "it?" Asked the women
As they made the customary three ululations
That heralded the birth of a girl or a calf;
I kicked my tiny legs in the air;
A violent objection to my objectification;
None paid attention, none cared;
For between my legs my fate was written;
An oracle, inerasable, a curse from the gods;
Who in their anger had denied me the wiggle, the worm; life;
And instead stamped me with shame; a tiny welt, an object.

They called me Wamathiina "she who carries sorrows"
For between my legs they read my fate;
"She is a woman and sorrow is her lot."
I was a happy child and brought joy to all;
But they did not call me Gakenia "she who brings joy;"
Like my mother, I had many talents too;
I could cook; lay the table, say the grace, do the dishes;
And pick after everyone else;
But they did not call me Nyawira, "the illustrious one;"
They called me Wamathiina "she who carries sorrows"
For between my legs sorrow was my lot.

They must have loved me no doubt;
My mother, my father, my brothers;
For did they not provide a safe haven in the kitchen?
A woman's sanctuary, her hallowed ground?
Away from harm's way, honed skills and manly games;
For who would dare gainsay the gods
Who charted my life's path between my legs?

We were a big happy family, or so they said;
But there was a large fly in the family ointment;
Papa Jeremiah who lived with us;
Rather sat with us, for he lived on a wheel chair;
His broken body grotesquely twisted;
A hero of the white man's war for a cause he did not know.
Every night I would take food to Papa Jeremiah's room;
A divine duty, honour to a fallen soldier;
The only homage I could pay to God and country;
My destiny, my fate, pre-ordained between my legs.

Papa Jeremiah would grab the tray and toss it aside;
His momentary fast belying his eager greed;
As his gnawed arthritic fingers possessed my body;
As if he would devour me with his food;
Suddenly his breathing would change;
And like a wounded animal, his guttural voice

would cry out in pain—"Wamathiina my sister's daughter;
You were created to make men happy;"
And like the thunder and lightening from the hills;
He would rumble, groan, foam at the mouth and go limp;
and push me away, angered by his act.

I would run to my room, confusion, fear and shame;
etched on my young face;
I could not tell Mother;
Papa Jeremiah was her favourite brother;
I could not tell Father;
Papa Jeremiah was his brother-in-law;
I could not tell my brothers;
Papa Jeremiah was their favourite uncle
And I was the spoiler, the bearer of the curse;
For between my legs sorrow was my constant companion.

They took me to a boarding school, away from home;
Away from Mother, Father, and my brothers;
Away from Papa Jeremiah and his primal games;
To a place of peace and quiet, drama, music, poetry;
Bible stories of a far away heaven;
A place I would go to if I was good;
And become an angel with wings to fly and my own tiny worm
Between my legs, free from the curse at last.

I joined Father Dougan's catechism class;
For only he could prepare me for heaven;
"God bless you my child" he would drawl
As his fingers in perfect synch with his laboured breath;
explored every bump, nook and crook;
of my rapidly changing adolescence;
The rhythm of stolen pleasure, the sensual dance;
He would lift his eyes to the hills on my nubile chest;
and in adoration to the god of lust would invoke the
     phallic blessing;
"Blessed is he to whom these breasts will one day belong."

I would run to my room and cry myself to sleep;
Confused, angry, defiled and afraid;
But I could not tell anyone;
For how could I lift my voice against the Lord's anointed?
Against Father Dougan God's messenger to a sinful world?
The man who served God's immortal body and blood;
To mortal beings to eat and to drink?
I carried my sorrow and shame in silence;
My destiny written between my legs.

At college I saw the light and learnt to fight back;
My epiphany from Wamathiina "the carrier of sorrows;"
To Wamathiina "the warrior of the sorrowing" was complete.
In men I saw neither friend nor foe;
But my Father, my Brothers, Papa Jeremiah
and Father Dougan rolled into one,
I fought with all I had;
Nails, teeth, tongue, pen and the alphabet;
I fought for me; I fought for others;
The curse between my legs spurred me on;
I came out victorious and unscathed.

At the beginning all was well at work;
Then slowly, subtly and surely;
The ghosts of Papa Jeremiah and Father Dougan
Started creeping in;
An accidental bump, a handshake that lingered too long;
A kiss stolen in a dark corridor; a word carelessly spoken;
An unnecessary trip abroad; a too generous Christmas gift;
Then the bombshell: Yes the promotion is yours for the taking;
But remember there is nothing for nothing;
A little love is all I need from you.

The courtroom was packed; it was D-Day
When I Wamathiina would redeem my honour;
And that of my sisters;
For in this court I had broken the culture of silence;
And here justice would flow like a river;
And with it carry away my sorrows.

Robed in dreadful majesty, powdered wig and clerical collar;
The apparel of his calling, justice to dispense;
The learned Judge beckoned me to the Bench;
From whence he spoke words of great wisdom;
"In the very beginning; God made Adam and Eve;
Male and Female made them He;
To work, to play and to live together;
In the discipline and practice of the law;
Naught would bar a man from playing with a woman;
For why would an all wise God create a woman but for
the just enjoyment of man?
Too much reading has corrupted your mind Wamathiina;
All work without play makes you a dull lass indeed;
In the journey of life, play you must, but play wisely,
CASE DISMISSED!"

Weep Not Mama Afrika

Weep not Mama Afrika;
For the Oracle has spoken,
And tomorrow the Sun will come out;
And the ferryman will leave your shores;
For in terrible majesty Musi-o-Tunya has decreed;
The Smoke that Thunders; the voice of the gods has spoken;
And the guns must go silent;
And listen to the careless laughter;
The joyous abandon of Darfur's untainted youth;
The song of harvest as Juba brings in the yams;
The dance of victory as Kivu returns home.

Weep not Mama Afrika;
For the Oracle has spoken,
And tomorrow the Sun will come out;
And the ferryman will leave your shores;
For the Great Lakes and their serpentine underlings;
The Congo, Zambezi, Mano and the Nile;
Will wash away your shame;
The menstrual flow of your disappointed womb;
The afterbirth of incompetency, seed expelled before its time;
And your sons and daughters; old and young;
Scavengers in strange lands;
will return to your bosom never to depart from you.

Weep not Mama Afrika
For the Oracle has spoken;
And tomorrow the Sun will come out;
And the ferry man will leave your shores;
For in an alchemic conspiracy, a sorority most potent;
Sangoma the Healer of Manyikaland;
Ajuoga the Seer of Nam Lolwe;
Thakata the Messenger of the gods of Azania;
Have found the elixir of life;
Death, a poisoned calabash to the curse,
The devourer of your daughters and sons;
The silent killer that defies the white man's medicine;
And tomorrow, the world will call you blessed;
The Mother of Nations; the Giver of Life;
For the small one with a big name—AIDS, SIDA, SLIM; *Kamdudu*
Shall be vanquished and banished from your shores forever.

Serah Mbatia

Giriama Peasant Woman

Gone too early is her childhood
Infants cling to her leso cloth
Resting on her lap is her newborn
It's going to be a dry season
Another woman walks into the compound; her co-wife
Mangoes in the basket weigh down on her head
Another stolen childhood

Placing the baby in her eldest daughter's arms
Eager to look into the basket
A sigh escapes her lips
So many children, so little food
A glance at the dry fields
Nothing to appease the rumbling stomachs
Tonight it will be mango soup for supper.

Willing milk from her tired body for the baby at her breast
Only a miracle can save them this time
Man of the house away in the city, looking for a job
All the rest are left to depend on her
Now she is the matriarch.

Lenah Mukoya

Drums and Sticks

They spoke of fear; of mockery and shame,
They told of the brave spear; of strength and fame,
I could tell it from the screaming skin,
From the hearts of my people,
came the songs of our land;

As the boys drained their fears away
at the glowing banks
and dewy sunlit grass,
I could tell they were tough as brass,
from the warrior song of the great mass;

While the women brewed their beauty in pots
and the old men told stories of sorts,
the girls danced with grace and might
and the boys recalled the great bullfight,
I swear it was joy I saw,
for I heard it from the songs of my people;

Bring some more skin
for the old is worn out,
hurry before the sun rests;
for how do I tell,
          of joy and sorrow,
          of fury and vengeance;
Tell me, how do I tell
          of the great harvest,
          of the great burial of the land,
for they are dead, my people;
The songs of our land are dead!

Connie Mutua

Harambee[*]

I.

I have raised presidents
given birth to
Kings and Emperors
immortalized their footprints
all over the pavements
Yet I am told
to stand in line
with the rest of my children
and patiently wait
for one of them
to decide
if I am a Queen.

II.

There are those of us
wearing the ties,
there are those of us,
sweating inside the veils
there are those of us
straying behind districts at night,
there are those of us
lining up the traditional brew,
and there are those of us
waiting like family jewels,

---

* *Harambee* is a Swahili political concept that means togetherness or the act of pooling re-
sources together for a common purpose.

Cooking
Baking
Making
And
Building the nation
behind prison bars.

III.
I am a face
chained to
duty and honor
seen only by the moon
and heard soothingly
in your sleep . . .
it is a puzzle
that I still give
—endlessly.

Sitawa Namwalie

Eh, Kumbe I'm Poor!

They told me I'm poor,
International experts,
Government ministries,
NGOs,
All sat together in conferences,
Wagged sad heads,
And sang in unison,
"You are poor
You live on less than one dollar a day!"

At first I dismissed them
Gathered an air of importance around me,
Told them *Kwenda Kabisa!*
I refute your claims
In fact I thrive,
I have all I need,
Luxuriant heritage,
Verdant calm,
Cool waters slake my thirst,
Did I not bequeath acres of land for your churches, your schools?
Just like that!
Are any of you as well-endowed as I?

The experts were adamant
They sang one song in unison
"You are poor
You live on less than one dollar a day!"

Led by the educated ones,
My own children joined the ranks of my doubters
I knew then I was lost,
They said, "*Baba,*"
"*You are poor,*
You have 500 Zebu cows?
Pahhhh! . . . a poor man's breed!
Humpbacked, misshapen, so thin!
Others, out there in the world, have, gleaming stacks of things!
In many shapes and colours!"
Guarded against the vagaries of life,
Coddled on feather beds,
They partake of rainbow tinctures
Transport themselves through richly seasoned dreams
Baba, your life is naked, elemental, without adventure
Your nights, deep, dark, relentless boredom!

My offspring coiled their lips at me!
Envy glinted their eyes,
They craved the history of others, coveted triumphs of strangers,
I was confounded!
To imagine,
I traded my wealth,
For this?
For progress?

Cowed by their dismissive disdain,
I dared not tell them the truth,
I never see a dollar any day!
Heh!
They would have declared me dead!

Whipped, shamed, with stinging verbal barbs
My laughter disappeared,
I started to see their point,
Indeed, poverty is all around me,
I feel . . . . drained,
Afflicted by strange maladies,

They attack my nerve!
Give me aches, pains!
Make me dissatisfied, depressed, listless!
I'm so without substance,
Small things flatten me!

The experts were adamant
They sang one song in unison
"You are poor
You live on less than one dollar a day!"

I lack so much,
Clean chlorinated H_2O, from a tap!
A modern highway, to take me anywhere
Power in my village
TV, microwaves, computers,
The emblems of a civilized life!

But, between you and me,
It's my children and wives, who worry me most,
Just too many!
What was I thinking!
Now they keep asking me for things I don't have
The experts were right,
Eh, *Kumbe* I am poor!

Mercy Ngigi

The First Cock Just Crowed

The first cock just crowed
And yet so cold, she slowly crawls out of bed
Everyone else is seriously snoring
That, she's used to ignoring
As she takes up her "mitungis"*
Before the day is as good as new
Like the grass dew.

She walks fast
Hoping to be the first
The first before the sun rises
Before the price rises
For the commodity is scarce
Though the consumers are a mass
But at a glance
This isn't her chance.

One by one, they queue
Like mothers who are due
They are in a hurry to get back
Get back, that their families may not lack
May not lack at least something to chew
And as they have a few patches of cloth to sew too
Then later make some stew for more than two.

---

* *Mitungis* is a Swahili word for the plastic containers, or "Jerrycans," that are used throughout Africa.

She takes it by the hand
To make what she will someday take
Someday take from the hands of nature
After the many she does nurture
With good sense and culture
Till they are grown into better stature.

As they came with no blame
They live with her and yet some bring shame
Others leave never the same
As their world is tame
As their world is no longer lame
And they can probably bring back a dame
To restart the well lived game.

Wandia Njoya

An Email for Antonio Jacinto

I'm sending you a message
across terrestrial and cyber space
to find you at your mailbox

I'm sending you a message
To let you know
That I miss your words
That carry me to a place I don't know, that I don't want to know,
     and that I enjoy not
knowing
That remind me that life is not built
by winning
but as friends, family, community, together
taking time to listen,
to ourselves and to each other
to the gods and to the ancestors
to nature
to silence . . .

I'm sending a message
to you that I saw on screen, heard on phone, read online
to you
that I dream, that I imagine, that I anticipate when
I open my mailbox
and find no unread message
to confirm or disprove my fantasies

Even though I'm not sure that you'll read
Or even if you do
What you'll think
Or despite what you think
That you'll answer
I'm still sending you
a message

Like I have done since the day
we met
on the internet
When war was on our minds
and we were worthy opponents arguing
about decisions that never included our input when they were made
but required our involvement to be carried out
And before long
Our divergent opinions brought us together
in a common search
of each other
of ourselves
of answers
that could change lives
and maybe one day
change the world

I'm sending you this message
for the work I begun
I will be, I will do my best to be
faithful
to complete it
until the day
I have no more faith to go on writing
no more soul to keep speaking

until the day
reality finally triumphs
over the dreaming part of me
still hoping,
wishing, praying
for a word from you

until then
I will keep sending you
a message

So

So you don't love me any more
I can deal with that
It's better than not knowing
Than waiting
Than wondering
Than not seeing your name
In my inbox

So you don't love me any more
I can deal with that
I can move on
Make plans
No more "We'll see"
or "that depends"

So you don't love me any more
I can deal with the pain
The tears,
the disappointment
Transfer you from "Pending"
To "Used to be"
Where there are others like you
Whom I knew, once loved
Until fate or I
Decided to move on

So you don't love me any more
I can finally cry
Heave a sigh
Stop holding my breath
Walk outside
Pretend my tears are the raindrops
My mood the grey skies
And my sniffles allergies

So you don't love me any more
The world still turns
Love is still beautiful
Business still usual
My smile still wide
So no one can tell
That you don't love me any more
I can deal with that
on my own.

Marjorie Oludhe-Macgoye

Diggings

You are looking for peace?
Peace in the Rift Valley, Bonde la Ufa,
where upthrust and downthrust,
fissure and subsistence, have created an awesome landscape
with habitable patches and abysses
concealing the cave of history.
Humankind crawled for millennia up the wall
hanging on tooth and nail to its birthright
until it splits.

Looking for peace? They burned it.
                            Search the ashes
For my baby's ear-ring, my husband's boots,
The bags of seed, the hymn-books, the flag
For Sabbath processions, the voter's card,
the basin and the gourd. Reconstitute
these if you think you can recover peace.

Peace? We have buried it.
                            The dog we slaughtered
to mark our boundary's come to life again.
The pacts we made are withered, like the leaves
we waved in promise. Marauding youngsters
eager to try their weapons represent us.
Suits and certificates have lured our teachers
away. Those who offered sugar and tee-shirts
might as well throw them, unworn, undigested,
into the ditch where body-parts and refuse
rot, swell and stink, uncovered, uninspected.

Peace? They have sold it.
                                        If you wish to buy
where's the container to conceal and carry
so perilous a purchase? Fancy cars and titles
are what they sold it for. Will they outlast
another round of talks, resettlements
and photo-opportunities?

Peace exists where people
count others greater than their single selves.
Proclaim it on the mountain, in the kiosk
at the street-corner, on the playing field,
unfractured, patent, whole, freely exchanged.
        It is not easy to come by,
        but hominid fossils, sediments of gold,
        glacial cores, ancient weapon-workings
        have yielded to our diligence.
                                        Keep looking.

Keeping Up with the Times

Growing old uses up too much energy
per unit of progress: we need a surcharge
on families that fail to keep their decrepit elders
off the overcrowded stage.

Your legs creak at the ankles,
coloured print dazzles,
minutes of mobile time whizz by
while you look for your glasses,
and the world spin pulls you apart.

Stem cell researches wiggle like worms in your ears,
GMO side effects clog your nostrils,
the crash of destabilized glaciers keeps you awake.
Then you think you hear dogs wailing, but more likely
it is the politically abandoned babies or Guantanamo non-prisoners
whose cries reverberate.
                                        Have you computed
the net effect of cremations on carbon emissions
compared to the firewood roasting the slaughtered cattle
at the burial site? How many airmiles
are consumed because a road is out of repair?

Pirates and identity thieves
are the new criminals, leaving no footprints.
somehow their DNA is not recorded.
                                        Habeas corpus
has gone out with the teaching of Latin. Old hat
like carbon paper and marital promises.
He stroke she stroke it has problems in filing forms.
Those detained are virtually answerable
to charges under suspended application
of an undated notice in vacant time.
Does this mean they are sacked? Divorced?
ineligible for benefits? responsible
for water charges and accruing interest?
                                        Limbo
has become a new district, and you need
the chief's signature on your pension application.
We long ago discarded rods, poles, perches,
furlongs, cents, guineas, florins, pice and farthings.
Now the new calculator makes equations.
Seventy five homesteads make one gold medal.

How many classrooms to a motorcade?
Is it five commissions to a received opinion?
How many smoking granaries to a famine?
A death commands no compensation.
                                        Home
is where you were displaced from. Energy
you must conserve to face the growing old.

Sarah Navalayo Osembo

When Daddy Had an Affair

When she often came around,
Often I wondered why daddy smiled so.
Sometimes a dark cloud in mummy's eyes flickered;
But I sang and played;
Perhaps still too young
The crack in my family's fine porcelain
To even notice or see.

At the end of the rains the flowers blossomed,
So did she, my eyes grew round:
I wondered why so suddenly she had to leave.
To the coast she went, so they said.
But daddy would go away for weekends too.
Business he said—money he had to make.
Right in his arms I'd jump on his return.
Mommy just looked and a stray tear I saw.
How lovely, dear me, I thought.
For love to blossom till one cries . . .
I was young I guess—
Innocent to the ways of the world.

When I grew up I came to understand,
Daddy had an affair and all my life had been a lie.
The dark cloud in mommy's eyes suddenly made sense,
The tears she cried every time he went away.
Alas-even a step-sister I have!
Why that lady blossomed now I comprehend.
The business deals and trips all add up:
And the crack has finally let up
And broken us all into tiny cutting pieces.

The lady at school counseled me for a while, you see.
Said with pity time will heal us, you wait and see.
Eight good years I have waited through:
And the hurt is still as fresh as new.
Every time daddy leaves through that door,
A dark cloud passes over my eyes,
A tear drops for those I love
And I know what's in me cannot be undone.

My mommy left, you see
Said she couldn't take no more nonsense from him.
I stayed behind for reasons I know best.
Then I think of her. I think of daddy. I want to vomit.
He knows not I know, but I know.
Every detail about his double life:
And I have all these secrets in me,
Simply because my daddy decided to have an affair.

Mimi Harriet Uwineza

Dear Fire

I am writing to you trembling
Shaking and mumbling
It's cold out and within
From wars and hunger
From dictators and tyrants

Dear fire,

It's cold up here
Thousand hills
A burden of mine to bear
With you within, I will dare

Sweet fire,

Your touch
Like a whisper
Light but deep
Wakes the hope to care

Dear fire,

My kitenge is so light
Shared by rebels
Devils you put to fire
Warm me back to life

Deep fire,

Eager for your reply
Before the devils of war crushes
Heal me to fight
Bring me to life

Sandra A. Mushi

Reflections

I am more than
My hips and thighs
I am more than
My lips and eyes
I am more than
My smiles and sighs
I am more than that
I am light
I am love
I am life
I am beauty
I am strength
I am laughter
I am respect
I am sugar and spice
I am pride and dignity
I am nakedness
I am a prayer
I am a blessing
I am the breathtaking reflection
Of God's love for me
For
I am God's child

I have taken my place
I have stayed
For
I have a choice

Clara C. Swai

"Happy New Year!!!"

Wait a minute dear,
Is this going to be a happy year?
Tell me, will my darling draw nearer?
My ears, sweetness to hear?
My lips much softer and silkier?
From kisses and touches so dear?
The kisses and touches of love; oh mama-mia!
Will my eyes have less to tear?
The kids, not my house to smear?
Nor my energy off to wear,
My spouse, never to swear?
And will my wallet swell up to greener?
My job become much easier?
My tasks not a burden too heavier?
Will I, my friends, be able to bear,
As they torment me with their bitter-sweet cheer?
Will my waist (cross my fingers) become slimmer?
My heels solid and higher?
My walk, graceful and sexier?
Will my smile grow broader?
My emotions more calmer?
From this January to December?
Tell me, my dear new year . . .
As we greet each other,
In this journey of life, alongside others,
Will the greeting "Happy New Year?"
Be responded to, with genuine cheer?
Will you really this year,
Deserve the name "Happy New Year?"
Am wondering . . . please answer me, my dear.

Monica Dorothy Aciru

Why Delay the Inevitable?

What man will want you?
When your head is full of knowledge?
When you carry all those books around?
When all you talk about is global warming; politics; philosophy;
    international this and international that?
When all you talk about are things beyond his head?

What man will want you?
When the "papers" he has do not even fill up your one hand,
And the "papers" you have, you need a whole box file
    or two to keep?
When his CV is hardly a page,
While you need to reduce the fonts and increase page margins
    to accommodate yours?

What man will want you?
When bills are not your worries,
And outings do not mean you need to wait for a man to call you up?

What man will want you?
When you choose to be choosy?
When you set such high standards?
When you choose to be educated, knowledgeable, strong
    and independent?

Why delay the inevitable by trying to reach for the stars,
When you can just touch the street lights?
Why does the inevitable imply compromising the best I can be?
Why do my successes have to be measured according to the
    inevitable?

Why does it have to seem like in pursuing my dreams, I am delaying
the inevitable?
Why must I put my life on hold until the inevitable happens?

If it is as inevitable as it is said to be,
Then it will still find me,
And it will not matter that I am holding the stars in my hands.

Susan Nalugwa Kiguli

Guilty
(Inspired by Mrs. Dorothy Ongom)

I was guilty at four
Of loathing our mothers' sense of diet!
They knew nothing save for
Flaccid vegetables,
Sinewy pineapples and tangy oranges.

I was guilty at eight
Of thinking that all our mothers were
Fashion gurus, beauty queens, story store houses
And boundless treasure haunts.

I was guilty at sixteen
Of regarding our mothers
Irrelevant, interfering women
With exasperating habits
Of mind reading, second guessing and disaster prediction.

I was guilty at twenty four
Of suspecting all our mothers
Of incurable matchmaking
Of approving the world's most infamous nerds
For boyfriends
Of reminding us of family obligations.

I am guilty now
Of constantly praying for
Our mothers' safe keeping
For hoarding all the cryptic comments
We received when ears heard
But hardly listened
For coveting the way they carry age like an accolade
For longing insatiably for their cooking
For their ability to prepare *Matooke, Malakwang* and millet
And to bake roast, cake and pie
For their defiance of hard times when
Sugar and salt were scarce
For their belief in their faith and values.
I am guilty of wishing to take all the soul
Of their generation to use it to redeem ours.

I am guilty of mother worship.

To War Mongers Everywhere

Tell us
Did you start a war
So our women
Could be sold to public shame?
Our girls everyday
Stripped bare of humanity
And treated to
Machinations of deranged soldiers?

Tell us
Did you start this war
As a trade fair of evil
Displaying the different faces
Of Lucifer to a terrified populace?
Our children naked holding guns
To their chests.

Tell us now
Did you design this war
As a catalogue of atrocities
To enshrine in the libraries of our history?

Did you engineer this war
To blaze us in the flames of your feuds
Or was it so you could issue official statements?

Harriet Naboro

Leave Me Alone

Go . . . go
Why do you send me away like a parasite?
We had these children
As an act of love

Go go go
I no longer need you
But consider what we have gone through
Now I have to leave alone

You are such a fool
You are very stupid
Let us talk, what do you think
I don't want; not that rubbish

Why father of my children?
Yes go today
I don't want you in my house
Okey dear, I will be Silausi's place

The original poem was written by Naboro using five different languages: English, Luo, Luganda, Lusamia, and Swahili. Translated by Harriet Naboro. The original version of the poem appears in the Appendix on page 172.

Patience Nitumwesiga

Created Woman

I don't want to be the kind of woman
Who spends her life wondering
Whether to obey or rule
I just want to be a free fair woman
Who neither rules nor obeys
I want to be fully human
Not the slave they made my mother

I don't want to be the kind of woman
Who wastes time struggling
To be like a man
I just want to be a proud honest woman
Who knows women and men are different
Never capable of acting or behaving the same way
Yet none less, none better than the other

I don't want to be the kind of woman
Who refuses to work
So her husband could be the sole breadwinner
Who cries to death because she has lost a man,
Who dies to be the traditional good woman,
Who cries silently, until she slowly dies away,
Who gets scared of divorce, because family and friends
Will disown her,

I don't want to be the kind of woman
Who rotes away in submission,
Asking for permission to be herself,
Who tells her sons they are more important and more powerful
Than women,
Who tells her daughters to do house work alone,
Who expects favors from men,
Who allows to be sold off at a cost of bride price,
Who gives culture as an excuse to keep her in her misery,

I don't want to be the kind of woman
Who believes the propaganda
Those mighty men have spread since the world began
That they own the female species,
That they rule the world.

Who loses her identity at marriage,
Who struggles to please her husband,
Forgetting her needs, and yet dying uncared for

I don't want to be the kind of woman
Who listens to sermons every day that all end up
Centered on making the world better for males,

I just don't want to be this woman the men have created
for themselves.

I want to be myself,
I want to play in the rain when I feel like,
I want to go out with my friends when I need them
Or when they need me
I want to take control of my life, the way my father does.

I want to cook when I feel like,
I want to find food on the table when I can't cook.
I want to see my sons and daughters share the same joy and pain
I want to see them respect each other the way my brother
never respected me

I want to unbelieve this myth
That God put the world in the hands of men,
I want to be loved for who I am,
Not for enduring what my grandmother thought was her fate.

I just want to be a woman
Who doesn't worry about her gender
I just want to find joy in being created female
I want to be the woman I was created to be
Not what the world has made.
I want to be me.

Beverley Nambozo Nsengiyunva

Microwave

The cold chicken stares back at me
almost Lifeless.
Dotted with pickles for eyes
and curry for mascara to mask the pain underneath.
It lies glazed with golden oil
and stuffed with potatoes and nonsense.

My cold house stares back at me
almost Lifeless.
Dotted with wedding photographs
and a new car to mask the pain underneath.
Honeyed with a kiss and sex
and stuffed with *I love yous* and nonsense.

I turn the heat on the microwave
and watch the chicken burn
                              and turn
I watch its skin scar
              like char.
It can't see or feel.
Its usefulness only for a meal.
The tenderness of the shower's heat
hits my skin like hot hailstones;
in readiness for my husband.

I Will Never Be You

I will wear my high heels to the market
so that I do not look like Mama Nandudu.
Her toes are always dancing with the stones and her feet are
    always kissing
the insects on the ground.

I will carry bananas in my car
so that my weave does not look like Mama Fina's.
Her hair is always squashed like my son's jam sandwich.
Her head is always sweating
like my back after the sauna.

I will not pay by cash but by cheque.
The scribbles with which I am worth;
My death, my life and my birth.

Unlike you, I will not thank my husband for that orgasm.
Instead I will silence my lips as they tremble against each other
like two slabs of jelly.
I will slap my thighs for betraying me
as they drip with longing for more.

I will never be you.

Jemeo Nyonjo

But the Rains Have Refused to Come

The weather forecast predicted the rains
The caretakers donated donated seeds
Generosity seeds from across the oceans
Seeds traveled a long journey on a ship
Seeds carefully packed for safe delivery
Seeds kept too long to be useful.

The caretakers said to have a fine queue
So order could be observed,
Time not wasted
Said to dip our left thumb in a purple ink jar
So no one receives an unlawful potion
Potion in one hand, dipped coloured thumb up
"That's a party signature" a voice in the queue
The order was disturbed then
"We can't be fooled into a bribe" an unorganised chorus . . .

The donations received, coloured thumb up
We tilled the dry stony land
A famished group, an anxious lot
We planted the seeds, waited for the rains
A famished group, a hopeful lot
But the rains have refused to come!

The Clinic

It is Thursday last
Every month
I visit this place
Sit on this bench
Or another of the kind
Sandwiched by those like me
Some better than I
Others much worse off
Waiting

In this place,
We come for health
To better life
Yet others lose it!

Jennifer A. Okech

I Say No More!

I say no more
To the inhumane *barga**
Forcing its way without knocking;
It stands and gives a fierce stare.

Without any warning,
You weave and cut me open:
You leave me clean
Making chronic urinary and pelvic infections
My lifetime companions.

I lay my body
You party on it
My labia minora and clitoris are extinct
Tradition dictates role of submission to me
Making me a perfect picture of misery
I say no more!
To the barbaric *barga*

---

* *Barga* is used by the author here to mean "dagger."

Hilda Twongyeirwe Rutagonya

Sometimes

Sometimes you want to sit in the inside of you
To speak and listen from within
Sometimes you want to hide behind you
To lie beneath the shadow of you

Sometimes you want to step out of you
To stand and watch from a distance
As the life boat swings past
To destinations unknown

Sometimes an image farther is clearer
Closer it merges with you
Sometimes
It becomes you.

I Hear Your Voice Mama
(Exactly one year after she passed on 17 September 2010)

I hear your voice Mama
In the hoarse winds brushing past
I hear your plea to be held
As pain climbed your every limb.

I hear you Mama
As you called out for your husband
As you implored us to turn you left from right
Martin's name swift on your tongue.

I hear your voice Mama
At noon on my desk
In the thick silence of the night
At day break with the cockcrow.

I hear you Mama
At sunset as I head for home
As I shuffle for keys to my door
And you, welcoming me home.

I still smell your scent Mama
From that last hug in Mulago
As you breathed your last
Three times it was, gone.

I still hear your voice
To my left, to my right
But today I release you
I will stand I promise,
Go in PEACE Mama.

SOUTHERN AFRICA

Botswana
Namibia
South Africa
Zambia
Zimbabwe

Cheshe Dow

Prologues

I don't read prologues.

That I put this, my fear of my impending silent death, a death to be mourned only by myself, in the prologue, is perhaps as much as I will ever tell you about who I am.

I don't know how it sounds to you to read me say this, but what I record here is my salvation. Some people get married, some have children and others find a way to believe in a God. For me, I need to know that I was here, that I was real before parts of the mask became my face.

When I was a child others saw me and remembered me. When I got old enough I asked to hear others tell of me as if I wasn't there. I asked often. Not because I didn't remember, but because I didn't want to forget.

I am suddenly gripped with apprehension that after this winter, I will not ask myself again what I really feel. And so before this my last childhood quits the stage, before I forget that, "it's not fair" is a damning recrimination I would like to answer myself on that worthy question and I would like to try to do it well.

I see my ability to claim that I am not complicit, my freedom to use "they" slipping away and I find that I want to rage, at least one last time.

You see, I am about to graduate from Law school and the natural evolution of things finds me being asked everyday, whether I have a job. In the face of this incessant questioning, I have decided to take the summer off so that I can hold on to my "theys" just a little while longer.

I see it coming fast, just this past weekend I read *Stone Butch Blues*, Jesse was raped twice and I didn't flinch until the second time, more than a hundred pages later.

One hundred and twenty-two days is all the time I have. I hope I didn't leave it too long.

Untitled 1

Just for an evening
I was free
I did not know his name
But by the first rays of tomorrow
He had known mine
Five times

I wish you could have been there
That evening
When I was myself
Not the magazine I had read that morning
Nor the sitcom I had watched that afternoon

I wish I could have stayed
There within myself

But
As the sun stripped
My reverie of its mantle of darkness
So did I take mine own up
Embroidered with guilt
Hemmed ever so surreptitiously with insecurity

And if you looked closer
You would see the little flowers
Adorning my mantle
Trying not to bloom too brightly
Trying to not let anyone see

That last night
I was free

Untitled 2

I can't help feeling that I should be in love
Or at the very least in lust
Before I can do justice to a poem entitled He
But since…

Moleta ngwedi o leta lefifi   She who waits for the moon
                                  Waits also for darkness

I will try then
to make use
Of these last moments of twilight

He . . .

He is what I thought I saw
But may never be sure
He is a fleeting instant
surrounded
On all sides
by what I have lived and what I now think I know
He is those last precious moments of bad posture
Before I look around and sit up straight
He is that moment in the dark accompanied only by
    the opening bars
He is the saliva sprinting to the back of my face
Before being rudely interrupted
By what I have put in my mouth
He is what I am talking about
When I am quiet

NAMIBIA

Monica Mweliya Nambelela

My Child's Child

My child the child of my child
My child's child listen to the somber story of my life
My child's child this misery started even before I became
    someone' wife
My child's child the number of children I beared this union
    stood at steady five
Very often I was close to having my throat slit with a knife
I did all I could to please this man I truly really strived
Every time he was cheating
Many times I got the beating
For every question I asked
I got bruises to nurse with a hot water flask
For every bruise I nursed at home
Not even the police dared to come
My child back then we had no voice
But now my child you have the choice
When every single dream of mine got shattered
That's when all I ever wanted stopped to matter
A white clad doctor gave me the news
My whole body felt the blues
Maaaam you are HIV Positive
Please live your life not negative
For now my child I am on medication
But the real miracle is called mediation
Give me no eyesore
When I close my eyes
Listen to my voice
Your choice shall be life
For the time for change is rife.

Nicole Elisha Hartzenberg

The Cats Snarl

The cats snarl
at the paled moonlight
Yes, they feel it too
The cold which has swept this land

into plunged ice
And its people
into woolen armour
weaved helmets and breastplates

The warmth
of oil heated metal
lasts only a second
and soon it comes again

the cold silence
which resonates at night
reminds us
that we have no power
over the season's flight

Nosipho Kota

Toxic Love

toxic love has left her bleeding.
toxic love has left her with a torn lip, a blue eye,
    and a raised forehead,
as if she has been hit by a truck.
poisonous love has left her with missing teeth,
swollen aching ribs, that makes it hard for her to laugh
    or cough or even cry.
dangerous love has left her with blood
in her hands,
in her jeans and
in her heart.

Bernedette Muthien

Once in Afrika

electric pylons
like sheet music against the sky
with the moon as full
as mona lisa's smile
speaking promises of desires still to come
heavens filled with stars & open armed vermilion sky
as broad as the ranger's smile
forever following the southern cross
& countless spoor
empty threats of taking me in
deep where i belong in leopard's undergrowth
& dappled sunlight
the envy of any hedonist
with a farm
on my continent

as i thank my xyz
for this jaunt in kruger national park
where a pride of lions killed a zebra
and her baby in half an hour's horror
surrounded by jeeps from private oxymoronic game farms
that left me yearning for adolescent apartheid detentions
that i could at least
qualify

Makhosazana Xaba

Preparing for a Dinner Party

Don't worry my friend
I'll introduce her as a friend, while not holding her hand.

I won't look into her eyes across the table
or let any of our body parts touch, not even once.

I won't even offer to dish out for her
or take from her plate the olives I know she hates.

Later when a smoker or two step onto the porch
We will stay put in the glaring view of the diners.

Even when your boss makes one of his jokes about "these people"
I will fake a smile cause I know just how badly you want this
        deal sealed.

My friend, what else do you want me to help with
Cause I truly want you to clinch this deal?

Oh, I know, we just won't come, that should lighten your load
I know this will mess up your numbers and gender balance,

But, don't you worry my friend, you are creative
you will find two other women. And, that deal is yours.

Gifts to the Sea

Today
I bid my wounds goodbye:
buried, forgotten, ignored, invisible, raw
and those proud-looking ones in varying shapes of scars.
I give them all to the sea to hold, bless and disperse into its expanse.

Wondering

When they blame Dr Manto Tshabalala-Msimang
for thousands of deaths and some wish her dead,
as they demand their rights to treatment
I wonder who they blame for unprotected sex,
what they think of their responsibilities
and what wishes they have for the ones they infected.

Chiseche Salome Mibenge

$55 from Q St. to Washington Dulles
on Memorial Day

The taxi driver I stop is happy to hear I am Dutch
he has studied at the prestigious ISS in The Hague
Shows me his Master's degree
and another from Maryland
in a clean manila envelope full of education
extracted for me to authenticate
Two Masters degrees . . .
and I drive a taxi . . .
Life . . . choices . . .
My friend is a Professor
We were students together 15 years ago

I jumped in front of his taxi right near the Sunday market
An Ethiopian
I know Ethiopians, have lived in Addis Ababa
when Mengistu was a terror and Ethiopians terrorized
A Gujarati I befriended at the new cupcake bar on 20th lived
    in Zambia
her son leaped on me at first sight, undid my blouse, patted
    my breast,
clung fast to my neck and dropped a cool string of spit
straight down my cleavage as she pulled him off
Explained sheepishly, surrounded by white Washingtonians:
He has an eye for our skin, blacks . . . especially women . . .
    He misses his *aya*[*]
I have this same response to Ethiopians
my eye is drawn to them first,

---

[*] An *aya* is a house girl or nanny.

Before the other races,
And it is a gentle gaze
I do not cling to them,
But I feel like they will not throw me off if I tried

It is true I do not speak to Ethiopians
But it is different in a car,
the proximity of the cab marks silence between two Africans
        as enmity
So I reveal that I was a child in Addis, and he says
your father was an Ambassador! mock reproachful
Affirmative: My father was an Ambassador
He is not so clever—even a blind fool
should recognize himself
This Ethiopian taxi driver looks at me
only when I tell him I have a PhD
I am coming to teach at a good American University and I am 31
We are riding through Georgetown,
and he chews his tongue slowly,
because it is unpleasant seeing me again, his ghost

Do you know a Professor? De Wit?
That's right . . . the man must be retired years . . .
That man loved me very much . . . I ate at his house . . .
I was a good student . . . exceptional . . . a father to me . . .
De Wit begged me not to go to America . . .
He told me it was not the dream I was expecting . . .
He offered me the chance to do a PhD with him
I was . . . special
But I was young . . . Why would I listen? But my friend listened . . .
He is comfortable now, an intellectual…his kids are intellectuals . . .
and you, you listened . . . look at you

We look at me
We look away from me
We drop the subject
it is painful for both of us
We move to the immigrant's feel good pastime
Pulling apart the things America prides itself on,
religion, family values and democracy
You will see religion in America is a cult . . .
people are fervent, but priests are not preaching the Bible . . .
They are coaching the congregation
teaching them the 7 best habits . . . how to be CEO of your life
I make the sign of the cross, saying solemnly
"the sparrow, the eagle and the holy dove"
just something I picked up in an Episcopalian Church
He is delighted
So you have seen for yourself!
Yes that's how we pray in America . . . You know what real faith is?
He is testing me now to see how smart I am,
Not how many degrees I have but really if I will be a smart
        immigrant one day
I speak slowly
Real faith is not easy . . . It's hard . . .
a full Church means the Priest is preaching pop culture . . .
real faith requires . . .
"Humility" we say this word together loudly
We do not look at each other as we say it,
but we are not surprised at our
synchronization.

ZIMBABWE

Isabella Jeso

Memorials of Our Redemption:
An Epic Poem of Zimbabwe

Book the First, Cycle I: Birth of a Prophet

And there was a dance
under the sea
She danced her dance
to the song of the sea.
It was the dance of the lion, that
she sang in her heart
And the sea danced
her dance
before the Lord of Hosts
at midnight
a cyclone pounding drums
on the waters above,
when the wailing began.
A woman seeking re-entry
to a whole continent
but finding herself trapped
in a tangle of human bones
under the sea
"Rachel wailing for her children
because they are no more."
And she remembered a mother:
"My son Justin. He was twenty-five,
you know. He said to me
from his hospital bed—
dying of AIDS,

'You know ma,
life is but a moment in time. . . ."'*
And the dancer could not recall
the rest of the mother's words,
so poetic in the first edition.†

The African woman
is Queen; not
in the eyes of the world
but always,
in the eyes, of her children.
"Rachel crying for her children
because they are no more."
Looking now at the prophet
whose staff hovered over the waters, once,
echoes of the wailing sea
running through her veins;
A procession of dancers
above, beneath and around her
appearing and disappearing in
the caverns of the sea
and the Lion was the Lord of the dance.

From that landlocked nation,
among "her people,"
on the tropical grasslands
where granite mountains
stood as pyramids and
granite boulders, blunt obelisks
of the pharaohs, or the ptolemies—.

---

* An actual exchange with a mom at an informal social gathering, but I changed her name
in the poem.
† The first manuscript of this poem (always a work in progress) disappeared from my con-
dominium in the summer of 1997, after I had had company there for an afternoon. What
is presented here is a retrieval of that initial poetic thought, and the subsequent writings
and rewritings of the work.

Yet,
it wasn't the wind-music
of the mountains that
"her people" sang.
They sang the music of the seas
with profound eloquence;
"elegance," she had called it:
The music of the seas
the music in the seas,
speaking in their veins
among sandy streams
that ran dry each winter.
The music of their veins
echoing the prayer
of the seas . . . for Rachel
whose children are no more.

She tore through the cry of the sea
with the force of an exploding earth
to the sun
from where she was confronted by
the knowing eye of the moon.
She saw too from there
that continent
whose forehead had an open vein.
It was a river
whose head waters lay on the chest
of the land—to the left—
as she lay
a perfect place for the heart
had the land been human;

and the river, now more
an artery than a vein
drained life out of the heart
oozing, past mountains and sands
where her children looked
for each other
with sealed eyes.[§]
And the wailing of the sea
reached the sun and the moon.

It was Mt. Meru
she wanted,
crouched beneath
the land's naked heart;
and her soul echoed the cry of the sea.

How did John the Baptist
spend his desert nights?
Did he watch snakes
catch rodents?
Or mountain lions
search for prey?
Did he watch God's throne,
or did he sleep
amidst those snakes, lions, and scorpions,
alone in the darkness of the wilderness?

But for the pulsating universe,
her questions went unanswered—
and she moaned
in a slow descending dance
from the sun
to omnivorous canyons
beneath the sea.

§ These lines, in the continuing writing and revisions of this epic poem, are from a poem published in *International Quarterly* in the spring of 1994.

These warring hands
with painted nails
paint no more.

The water was playful that afternoon
the sky, a chopped-up sea
the blue of very deep clean waters
and the new leaves,
red like blood,
stood
their hands touching
in prayer—
spring had come.

But she moaned
in a slow, descending dance
from the sun. . . .

Who then is this
that stands with me
on the onyx rock,
always fanning, fanning his hands
like wings that war,
never uttering a word,
never assuming peace—
eating is war
dancing is war
procreating is war
teaching is war.
Teach who?
Your children, blah—blah—blah.
Does it matter
who wars beside you?
It matters more
who wars inside you
and through you ____ in places reserved for God.

How then to find
the way inside me;
whose life asserts itself
through me
in this slow war dance
on the flight to a continent
that bleeds into the sea?

Teaching is war.
Dancing is war.
Eating is war.

In the Hands
of a warring God
I dwell.
In His fiery Love
I burn with ecstasy.

WEST AFRICA

Burkina Faso
Cameroon
Ghana
Nigeria

Nathalie Hoblebou Ouandaogo/Rouamba

In Honor of Child Soldiers

Why can't I see the day?
Why can't I see the end of the tunnel?
Why this endless night?
These noises that whistle in my ears.
My heart that no longer recognizes any light.
My heart that rejects justice.
This heart that scorns the truth.
This heart that refuses to beat.
Is it mine?

Translated from the French by Janice Spleth and Nathalie Rouamba. The original version of the poem appears in the Appendix on page 173.

Poem: Bitterness

This feeling of guilt holds me by the neck
and won't let me go. What did I do? Can I
be wrong? Should I beg for pardon? Am I
really guilty? Who is actually wrong? It's a
difficult question to answer when one is
asking.

Survival, an instinct that often pushes us to
extremes, the only goal is to save your skin
at the cost of lies, betrayal and even murder.
I blame: man; society, the real torturer, the
subjective judge who perpetuates these
turbulent moments.

Friend! I am looking for you. In your eyes I
had discovered a marvelous world. Although
I search carefully, I still can't see you on the
horizon. Were you a mirage? You seemed so
real, unique in this darkness.

Translated from the French by Renee Hardman and Nathalie Rouamba. The original version of the poem appears in the Appendix on page 173.

Joyce Ashuntantang

Incantation

I sit by her side on a snowy day far from our girly days
When the sun's rays bathed our bodies
And our breasts were just body parts.
Her bald hair doesn't scream "chemo"

She looks like a glamour star
A cross between Sinead O'Connor and Alek Wek
Pain has purified her body—and she is holy
Her stories are incantations

Like her head, her memory is clean
So she tells of that night of seduction with Dina Bell[*]
Under cheap lights in a dusty student room
Her breasts now mangled, were juicy lemons then.

His hands found them, squeezing them jointly into his mouth
Beneath him, she danced to "Nyuwe",[†]
Directing him to the seat of her soul
But he ate her body and spit the rest

That's when the cancer began
The next morning she put an "X" on the picture of cupid
Above her six-spring vono bed
No more prayers to foreign gods

---

[*] Dina Bell is a Cameroon musician reputed for his slow romantic melodies.
[†] A popular song by Dina Bell.

Today pain cuts her breathing
And she talks between gasps
Tomorrow I will come with a notebook.
Pain knows how to tell
A
True
Story

Birth-Day

I was asleep son when you came
You did not see my eyes nor hear my voice

When I held you son, pain tattooed my body
And my nipple fumbled in your waiting mouth

I had no mother by me as should have been
So no pepper soup to wash my bleeding womb

How can I tell you son,
The wings of love did not fly at first sight?

That I was an alien in a foreign land
Lost in the thicket of lonely tears?

But Son, in the cushion of my arm
You gulped the prayer from my heart

Now at 15 questions abound as manhood
Prances on the edge of the boy

But some truths you will never know
You were not born with a womb

Lydia E. Epangué

First Snow in Africa

It came when nobody expected it,
When all in Africa was green and fit.
It first fell in Egypt and then spread.
The young were excited but old men feared;
For this snow came when Africa was at its peak.
Destroying all the beauty and pride of its green.
At first the snow drops were slow and weary.
Then they came in their numbers; fast and dreary.
Like the frogs invading Pharaoh's palace,
It covered most of Africa's surface.
This winter was tragic and devoured all of Africa.
Save for two that survived the snow—Liberia and Ethiopia.
It was Africa's first and last snowfall,
Famous for being the longest winter since Adam's fall.
It came just once, but has left unforgettable scars;
Traces and stains that'll forever be in every true African heart.

Mamazon

If she were an element she'd be Land,
Because like her, all other elements spring out of Land.
If she were a time, she'd be Dawn.
A bright yet gentle surge of colourful emotion,
Splashed across the sky like a promise waiting to be claimed
The mere manifestation of her presence foretells hope.
If she were in the Bible, she'd be Esther.
For beauty and grace make her remarkable.
If she were a tree, she'd be a palm.
Fearless and brave it stands out in the open,
Subjugating adversaries in the Winds, the Rains, the scorching Sun.
If she were a colour she'd be a deep dark forest green,
Bursting with potential as she embodies its natural beauty.
She's the woman who would go to war and take her household
    out alive.
And when she finally hands over that baton,
Mamazon will soar like a star to watch over me.
And it is not a gravestone I shall place over her head.
It shall be a Crown.

Thérèse Kuoh-Moukoury

The Lost Throne

Long ago is the time
Where I was sitting on your knees
Your breast, a beloved back support
Was carrying the weight of my childhood years
Before my eyes, the corn turned to dough
Through the effort of your arms,
My most secure armrests.
In vain, I search the world over
The warmth of this lost throne,
In vain, the softness of your back,
First universe that my arms embraced
In vain, the image of these backwaters
Where, for the children of Africa
You transformed yourself into a washerwoman
You were singing, joyful, among other goddesses of the shadows
A wild mango was swept away in its fall
A silent crash and a swarm of children
I rushed up, you shook your head
It's all over now, this I know
But I carry forever
The imprints of your breasts on my chest

Translated from the French by Cheryl Toman. The original version of the poem appears
in the Appendix on page 174.

Dance

I wore my dress of cowry shells
Come forward black man
Man in the iron mask
Man in the wooden mask
See my ebony skin adorned in raffia
Look, admire, the pearls
Shimmering on the necks of your wives
I am the chosen woman of the day
The promise of the gods
My heart filled with desire watches for the mysterious night
Here in the ancestral *pagne*, I am dressed
Let's dance the Yabo ritual, let's exchange our passion
The silhouette of my gazelle-like legs projects amidst the walls of
    straw-covered houses
And your weightless shadow slips between the fireflies
Let's dance the Yabo, the divine dance of our fathers
Let's dance the Yabo, let's dance
Soon the rooster's call will bring our dance to an end

Translated from the French by Cheryl Toman. The original version of the poem appears in the Appendix on page 175.

African Art

Africa
I love your music
    your sculpture
    your painting
I recognize myself
In these heroines of your past
I resemble these women
In your stone paintings
Were they from the Congo rainforest
    from the steppes of the Sahel
    from the Adamaoua mountains
    from Lake Tanganyika
I resemble them!
My soul etched on their faces
Recalls a golden age
Where my heart loved and suffered

I love your sculpture
Your statues of wood, of clay, of ivory, of gold
Forever set the human being in the magic of
Beauty
Pleasure
Power
On the fringes of eternity

Translated from the French by Cheryl Toman. The original version of the poem appears in the Appendix on page 175.

I love your music
Similar to the birth of the world
It alone, in collusion with time
Tells the sorrows of our hearts
In a language richer than words
Heat, Sun, Light
Oh tam-tam tam! Tam-tam tam!
Oh music
Suspended on the strings of the mvet
In the sounds of trumpets
On the fingers of the flutist
In the divine voices of the sirens, goddesses, and angels
African art, African art, your song: an eternal poem

Makuchi

Invisible

she stops
momentarily bowed
and lets them pass

purses, bags, briefcases,
hand luggage, wheeled past Her

a rusty door creaks
harried stilettos squeak
to the tune of tapping toes

a deep sigh
marks their spot
at the end of the queue

the line loops along walls
world-weary eyes snake down its spine
a rare moment when Her hem invites a glance

a dirt-pick's wooden shaft
snuggles in Her armpit
a brush's brown bristles
sweep up against Her blue dress

she Wheels the bin
she's Learned to protect it
and her White apron's trim too

sorry!
'scuse-me!
tap tap tap
those relentless heels
those flailing arms
those bodies that do not halt

for Brown hands that do not falter
arthritic limbs of a nostalgic Warrior
sheathed in Yellow plastic gloves

She stands, invisible
somnolent eyes, Her priced possession,
wearing Her sclerosed body
like sun-bleached Batik

She longs . . .
For the cry of the hyena
She longs . . .
For the dance of the hummingbird
She longs . . .
For the hoot of the toucan
She longs . . .
To stand in the market place

She can hear the cacophony
Reaching over the hills
Echoing across the grasslands
And she longs
            to whip out her Breast
            to Suckle the hunger
            till her Teats bleed

her sister vacuumed your lint encrusted floor
her brother handed you your encoded plastic key
her cousin placed chocolate-mints on your pillow

how often we stride
under the sign

and those sapped eyes
those arthritic hands
that sclerosed body,
elude us

those veined hands
dyed of piss and shit
those sightless eyes
yearning for home, hearth, rest

Away, planes soar
Alone, she treads
Aching, for mother-father-land
Home is here, beneath her aching feet.

American Dream

I walked in there
For a piece of paper
Signed, stamped—TB FREE

Needle pricks of yesteryears
Had branded me for life
My left arm sports the scar

Look, I said;
pockmark in full view
Why am I here?

INS commands it:
infected aliens
contaminate the salad bowl

Name?
Age?
Place of employment?
Race?

Race?
Cameroonian.
I said, "Race."
What?
R-A-C-E

What you mean?

. . . *your* race . . . *Ma'am* . . .

Her blue eyes piercing my skin
Cold, unflinching

Didn't know how to tell her
I've never been asked this question;
Never

Did she by any chance
Notice my confusion
Would she by any chance
Did it matter

And then I understood the legend
why the Rift Valley split open
And then I remembered
why frogs fell from the heavens
And Lake Nyos burped lethal fumes
Smothering her children

Ma'am?
Ah ain't got all day, you know
Don't you stand there
Looking at me
Like you ain't heard what I asked you

O Land of the Free
Where race is a tree
And i a trace
Etched in black on white

Frida Menkan Mbunda-Nekang

Oral Tradition

Feed them.
Let them suckle and be revived,
For the western wind is blowing.
Blowing anew,
Blowing dirt and dust,
Suffocating.
Masquerading as
Globalization.

My Mother

She rushes out before dawn and
Is back only at twilight,
Always in a hurry.
Day by day
To and from the field,
Climbing giant hills.
In rain or sun she toils,
Planting, weeding and harvesting
To feed the chauvinists
That despise her.
Her face drenched in sweat
Glitters in the sun as
She smiles and labours on,
A Rose she is to all.
She responds to every greeting
Even stops to gossip.
To the cheerless she offers a smile
To the hungry, a mussel.
When she appears,
Wrapper on her waist,
Basket on her back,
She is always a beauty to behold

Rosalyn Mutia

Ode to Feminist Criticism

Oh Feminist Criticism!
Thou light bearer of literary revolution
Gliding through the predictable agenda
Of ideological enunciation

Then prancing majestically to ordain
The Authority Giants
Who henceforth ascertain
The icons of the normal

But oh! the obsolence of normality
Amidst the glamour and the assiduity
Of New Generation Critics, the Dons
Redefining literary canons

How I love your trajectory
From apprenticeship to superannuation
Thou art an anomaly in the history
Of Literary Criticism!

Pat T. Nkweteyim

I Celebrate Me

You say I am weak
Me, the weak vessel!
You sure are kidding
I am me and you are you
I celebrate me for what I am

A cedar ever green and strong
Bringing ecstatic releases to many
The baobab resilient to all storms
Inspiring confidence and love in all

Sat on, buffeted and battered
A ladder to go up was I to some
And to others a board to write on
Yet like the sign post I stood still
Tall
          Strong
                    Directing all.

In perilous times a shield I am
A truck loaded with pleasant goodies
The manager, supplementing, galvanizing
Mother, wife, teacher, bundled in one.

A strong tower supporting the strong. Ha!
A healing balm soothing all pain
The great nanny when age sets in
With great wisdom uniting all

Yes I do celebrate me
For the wonder package that I am

They Came

Crush! Crush! Crush! Crush!
Heavy boots on gravel trod
Stern masked and cold faces appeared
They came in tens
They came in hundreds
They came in thousands

Brac-kata! Brac-kata! Bwoom! Bwoom!
They scattered in the quarters
Like birds on tree tops
They beat us as you'll do a snake
They broke our homes and looted us
They caught our sisters
And they were raped—oh!

Pitter-patter! Pitter-patter!
We fled in terror
As it was all horror
We screamed as we ran
Many fell on the way
And were fettered for sure
They were taken away in trucks

Aaugh
We deserted our homes
We became like paupers
We were like orphans
For they asked us to leave
They said we should GO HOME
After years of living here
They said we did not belong

Crush! Crush! Crush! Crush!
But how can this be
With our cords buried here?
Like lions we shall be bold
And fight for our rights
Till the last drop of our blood
We shall fight indeed
'Coz we truly BELONG HERE

Epifania Akosua Amoo-Adare

In(ner) City

Imagine this place;
brick walls sky high,
barbed wire,
and
you can't get over it
unmarked.

Imagine, then, this place;
no sun
creating shade from leafy boughs
dancing in a gentle breeze.
In fact,
no trees to complement an imaginary sun;
its stunning rays
seeping,
warming
your darker melanin clothing.

Imagine the people,
if any,
turning pale backs
along grey pavements;
cracked,
neglected,
smeared.
The people behind walls;
running quickly in
locking their doors
fearing conversation,
which means they're alive
and

can contest
those walls
those barbed wires
those pavements
that excrement.

Imagine this:
realize,
it's not just a figment;
having looked down your street
having walked sunless
having no people to share
your need
to get out/make anew.
But still,
having, perhaps,
HOPE.

Nana Nyarko Boateng

Abolition of Childhood

I write from hell
as heaven's proxy
mothers shall push babies
no more

let them walk out on their own
and when the umbilical cord is cut
strangle them with it

If, they do not die
or do not cry
when you hit their butt
they have become adults

now, tell them about sex
no, just fuck them
be their mirror as they shave-
off innocence

do not speak
to your child
but buy them toys
or let them play
with their spittle

mothers shall have no milk
and fathers will be busy feeding
theirs to other women

hang a picture of love
on your fridge till it freezes

children will learn to dance to their cry
as they skip around and pee
like baby goats do

NIGERIA

Toyin Adewale-Gabriel

Sister Cry
(for Nigeria at 50)

We are women of the corn rows plaits,
Wrapper rooted, song strong, waists fastened with determined cloth.
We are herstory, our stories sit in our wombs.

Sit beside me and hear the story of Amina.
Warrior queen, lover woman.
Amina, her stallions cry. Amina, the kings quake.
Where Amina is your well of knowledge to slake the thirst
    of the *alimanjeri?*
History now serves your milk with bitter *kunu.*

I am dream walking in the courts of Moremi,
Iya Afin Moremi who loves you past your pain.
She carries you in her spirit, she prays for you more than
    she prays for herself.
Lioness of Ile-Ife, she knows the analysis of tears: iron and
    strong bones.
When the masquerades taunted, where the fires raged, there
    she stooped to conquer.

Tell me of Olufunmilayo, Kuti's wife
Iya Abami Eda. Funmi of the owl-rimmed glasses,
    white man's terror
She would beat her breasts, drive the thread thin paths,
    past the tobacco seller,
Past the no-no gate, cross the demarcation of sex, till our
    voices are heard on high.

See the elegant Margaret Ekpo,
Teaching us the saga of the vote, urging us to the steering of
     the ship of state.
We need to come to each other in this time of wilderness,
In this high day, this tumultuous sea, when the wind passes,
     churning bitter leaf soup.
When the day is crusted with fuel scarcity and children out of
     school, the air pungent with VVF,
this high day of wild birds, moaning the women lost in the
     labour wards.

This is Ngozi's day. Iweala's time.
Sawaba strides in, Gambo, talakawa mother,
asking for what we must give, a sacrifice of gold,
a basket of courage, a strident voice.
We need to hold our scrap-iron nation, gutted in the arms of men
Between your body and mine is our womanity.

Oghomwensemwen Aimie Adeyinka-Edward

Immigration

Wide Eyed Expectations
Packed in tin suitcases
Checked into a plane that will take you
To the land bristling with rubies and rhinestones.

Your two feet taxi on the ground of the place that is your escape
From disease and corruption
Your heart races and speeds up with excitement as
You wait for the diamonds to fall on your lap.
Mistakenly you believe that disease will become
A memory past and finally forgotten.
You do not realize that sickness permeates the bodies of all lands.

Years come and years go
Your reward is a green card for the green land.
You now have the right to belong
Still your speech is corrupted with rolling r's
Your question:
"How are you?"
Is answered with the words:
"Where are you from?"
In order to make your citizenship authentic
You adopt their ways,
From their clothes to their food and you even adopt their heart
At the end you have forgotten that losing yourself in the transition
Does not mean you belong

The Fear of Broken Dishes

I'm not afraid of breaking dishes anymore
like when I was six
I would stand over the broken pieces
Thinking oh dear mommy will kill me
Mentally I would calculate
How quickly I could put on
Three pairs of shorts before
The strokes came down on my behind

Now I'm just afraid of the boys who break your heart
You know the ones you love selflessly.
Who make you do the things you swore you would never do
and even inspire you to change your cell phone network
Just so you can talk for free at odd hours of the night
But although you've done everything right
They end up breaking your heart because they were only fishing

I'm not afraid of schoolyard bullies anymore
like when I was seven
The ones that beat you up for the sport of it
So they see you cry and laugh for the fun of it
Now, I'm just afraid of government house bullies
The ones that steal for the greed of it
So they can watch the helpless
Silently suffering because of it

I'm not afraid of the dark anymore
like when I was eight
Whenever I was in bed and the lights went off
I would pull the sheets over my head
Imagining all the creepy things that crawled in the dark

Now I'm afraid that the darkness will never fade
The darkness caused by the ministries
Of unfulfilled contracts and siphoned oil cash
I'm afraid of the darkness of ignorance
Ethnicity against ethnicity
Using marginalization as an excuse
But evil has many languages and shades
It doesn't take increased quotas
To make the world a better place
It only takes a willingness to show grace

I'm not afraid of failing secondary school
Like when I was fourteen
Because daddy would put you in holiday lessons
Mom would cut your hair to free you from distractions
That caused you to ignore your books
And both would take away your TV watching privileges

I'm just afraid of failing as a human being
To whom much is given, much is expected
I'm afraid of dying and everyone asking why cry
She wasn't worth her salt anyway
I'm afraid that my fears will frustrate
Any ideas I had to do good.
I'm afraid of trying
Even though I'm no longer afraid of the dark
The fear of life still cripples me.

Akachi Adimora-Ezeigbo

Flint
(Song of Nneuwa)

I
A one-eyed loafer
waylays me in a deserted marketplace
hijacking my clothes
the shroud of my dead children
fathered by jackal rapists

II
His smelly mouth dribbles
spade teeth nibble my point-down breasts
the swollen gourds of the market god

III
His callused hands
grasp and squeeze my buttocks
the calabash of kings that never reigned

IV
Crooked pincer fingers
pinch my uncoiled navel
umblical cord buried deep below my life tree

V
Cymbals of bile and fire, potpourri of hate
saliva, salt water to the kill
rises to my palate, venomous

VI
My raging elbow lashes out . . .
connecting with naked groin
then a roar rents the air

VII
My aggression a red hot ember
igniting a conflagration
scorching his lust

VIII
The sting of the *agbusi**
dwells richly in its tiny body:
I jet out before he rallies

---

* An *agbusi* is a small black ant with a deadly sting.

Omofolabo Ajayi-Soyinka

The Code of Exile

Untie the bows
Unpack the box
Out with the old
Begin Again
My past a bargain

In this here bag,
My dreams I pack
It's check out time
From this deadlock life
Yonder beckons

Each day
Through the blur
I bring out the box
Repackage it in neat
Bows strings and paper

Each night
I unwrap the box
Lay it aside to recharge
My mind wanders home
Come morn the bows are out

Then one day
The stench hits,
I cut to the rotten mess
Inside and throw it all out
Now, I answer only to *my* name

Untie the bows
Unpack the box
Throw it all out
Begin Again is
The code of exile

My Christmas Wish List

The season of giving
The season of receiving
The season of wishes to fill
Christmas rolls by again.

My needs are rare,
My list is long and plenty
Though none can be bought
None is for sale at a store.

Every item on my list
Has been uniquely crafted
A powerhouse of integrity
Confidence and compassion

Tell me
How much does caring cost
What price do you put on generosity
Which designer shop peddles patience
Where can you order friendship and love

If you knew how much you
    keep me sane
    keep me strong
    keep me going
    keep me grounded
with your unconditional love
you would know I do not
need any other list for Xmas.

The three of you, daughters,
Are my perpetual gift-list
Since you came to this earth
Wailing, out of my womb.

Umma Aliyu Musa

World Genocide

What fate called me a minor?
For a cause
Of which I have no hand
A skin color that sold me off
To bare my back on labor to the sun

In blood we fought for freedom
In death we got the freedom
As no peace can bring back
Those moments of destruction
That forever parted us
From our soil

Amidst cigarette smoke and flowing ale
Decisions unfavorably were made
Nincompoop I was viewed
Then passed on to guillotine

And then centuries rolled
As modern age flew past
Still a minor I was viewed
Because my color made me a slave

Temitope Azeez-Stephen

Funeral Theme

Stop all the clocks, cut off the telephone lines,
Prevent the dog from barking with a juicy bone,
Silence the pianos and with muffled drums,
Bring out the coffin and let the mourners come.

He was my north, my south, my east and my west,
My working week and my Sunday rest,
My friend, my father, my foe and my family,
I thought that he would live forever, but I was wrong.

The stars are no longer wanted, so we hail them goodnight,
Pack up the moon and dismantle the sun,
Pour out the ocean and sweep out the woods,
For even the angels cannot bring him back.

Unoma Azuah

Umunede: Molding Memories

Umunede crawled and
Flickered its tongue
Like a rattle snake

Her wells gulped
The fury of storms

At crossroads
Calabashes bore offerings; they
Cracked the face of dawn

The slashes of knives on necks
Bore screams; and tore through town like
A cloth ripped

But mother hastens to her duties
Floating across frowning forests
I trail her

She teaches with chalk in her eyes
She shades her eyes with white dust
The white eye of the town stares at her

But she slides through the forests
Until we get home
Where rest and recesses reside

Leisure sends me on an errand
And a boy dangles yellow mangoes
He makes a tree top the table of our conversation

His fingers read a map on my thigh
But like thunder
My brother rumbles and rolls in

He carries me
Head high home

Where my mother's hands
Wag like a dog's tail
She tongues curses and incantations
They hang like dry cherries on drooping trees.

At noon play, the next boy
Hurls me into spaces swelling with sin
His rhythm soaks with sweat and
I claw at my crown of thorns

Days tie me up
Time refuses to untie me
My grandmother gropes for the ropes.

T. Mojisola Bakare

Dreams from a Kitchen

Sitting in this tiny, lonely kitchen
I dream of those places once again
Places filled with ladies with fully made up faces
Wearing short lovely skirts
Crisp ironed shirts with shiny wavy hair
Holding leather folders, talking, smiling
Slim mobile phones dangling
Between red painted fingernails like talons
Sitting behind mahogany desks, brown and polished.

My dream is cut short as I remember
That Grandpa said those lovely skirts I dream of
Make the tongue too sharp
Those shadow colored eyes I long for
Make you belittle your husband
And lose respect for his mother
The ideal is to learn
How to pick the driest woods in the forests
Kindle the best fire
And serve the most sumptuous soup.
So I deal with the ideal
My eyes see only the ripest fruit
My hands pluck it not a second before its time
I make homemade soap and save him the extra expense
I make the meals and keep the household happy.

Yet I still dream all day in my trap of a kitchen
As I watch them go by in the morning
Those ladies in colorful cars decked in multi colored apparels
All shades of colors accentuating their eyes
Going to those places
Places in the hollow of buildings almost stretching into the skies
And I wonder how many
Razor-like insults dwell in those gloss coated mouths
And how many mother in laws have fled
At the sharpness of the bite within

Once or twice I tried to paint
My nails blood red like the cute ladies of my dreams
But soot from my blackened pots
Wrecked my efforts in less than a minute
Mascara on my eyelids almost caught fire
As smoke and heat from my beehive of a kitchen
Smothered my face with black tears, stinging and tingling.
So I keep my kitchen warm and busy
My dreams subdued but still coming
His mother happy and dandy
His heart fulfilled and blissful
That one day our daughters glad and cheerful
May see those places I only dream of.

Not a Slave

He calls to her as she mends the clothes
Left in a pile at her feet by his son
Her fingers pricked by the needle bleeds
Rumblings in her stomach remind her
Of yet another breakfast missed
It's lunch hour, he says
Baked glazed chicken, pasta and not to forget the martini, he orders
But he fails to notice as she rises to answer his call
The proud tilt of Maria's jaw.

She calls to Maria
As she scrubs the doorway clean
Her knees, bruised by the hard stone floor hurts
The dryness in her throat reminds her
Of that cup of tea now cold and sour
There's silverware to be polished and set
The Mayor should arrive soon, Madam says
But her eyes missed and detects not
That graceful angle of Maria's shoulders
As she steps forth to do her bidding.

Then she sings that song softly under her breath
As she goes through her chores one after the other
That song that reminds her
Of the richness of her own native tongue
Of the dung filled air of her father's farm
An unbelievably pleasant contrast it has become
To these sweat fed plantations.

That song that soothes babies
Tied dangerously yet shockingly secured
To their mothers' warm back
Mothers running to the stream
At the first sign of the early morning sun
To fetch blue brown water in homemade earthenware pots
Mothers with natural plaited weaves
Adorning black, glistening scalps
Undecorated models of the magic abound
When feminine fingers meet the arts

Maria in her mind
Would trade the elegance of this intimidating mansion
And exchange the alluring sights and sounds
Of this so called God's Own Country
To taste the starchiness of homemade cassava balls
To wrap that fabric, tied and dyed
Under her plump, brown arms
And balance that woven basket on the centre of her head
On the way to the evening market
And break free from the chains of this ill-fitting, unbefitting apron
The remnants of an unspoken treaty
Long dissolved, long discarded
By the sacrifice, the blood shedding
Of black heroes past and rested
Selfless, fearless, relentless brothers
That the future may witness sisters
Who shall walk and live free

The first ring of Madam's bell
Jolted Maria back to the present
But along came another ring in her head
A consciousness of where she should be
A remembrance of who she should be
The uncelebrated uncrowned heiress
Of an enduring race, black proud
Perpetually culturally endowed

As she hands the martini to him
The veins in Master's hand look the same
As Papa's
As he dug his hoe into the loamy soil
Somewhere on the plains of Jos
And when Madam lifted the silverware out of her hands
Her fingers looked the same
As Mama's
As she ran them through the loom
In that smoke filled yard
Somewhere far faraway to the West of the Niger
I'm not a slave, she whispered
For an inner light glowed inside her, out of the blue
As she unfastened and dropped the ill-fitting apron
Maria picked her glory and freedom.

Damilola Balogun

Freedom Farce

We skipped along paths
Humming rhymes of joy
Carefree, oblivious of what
Loomed ahead

We were paid a visit
By scarecrows in khaki shorts
Pandemonium broke loose
Brothers sold their freedom for mere
Vain objects only to discover their entrapment
like the bush meat caught

In the hunters trap
Bound in chains that couldn't be broken
We were carted away like grass cutters

Blood fights, deaths of heroes ensued
We chanted songs of freedom
Alas! The victory ours
We had what was ours

Unknown to us;
A menace had crept in
Among us like blood thirst
For power that destroys

The very ones who
Were to bring back
Fond memories of our existence
Before the strangers came in

Dealt us blows that paralysed
Our muscles into inactivity
We were trapped like the hunter turned prey
We have since lost the fight

We are all prisoners
Of the virus that has eaten us
Like weevils in bean seeds
We had thought all we
Needed was freedom but we've been
Trapped by our very own deception

Love Chioma Enwerem

Will Long Be Gone

When from slumber
Your heart awakes
Far, so far away
From desperation
Looming over you
Longing for the smiles
You turned away from
The light blown off
In a hurry and fury,
I will long be gone.

When the heat
Of your passion
Subsides
Dropping fantasies
On your drowsy heart,
Desperately you search
For once scorned care.
Like a drenched fowl
You run for shelter
In the arms you ridiculed,
I will long be gone.

When beads of salty sweat
On your forehead
Turn to stream of tears
And your heart
Beats like a raspy drum
You will look for the
hands you pushed away
Years ago
To wipe your tears,
And soothing words
To cheer you up,
I will long be gone.

They Call It Hurricane

It came like the wind
And hurled at us with fury,
We turned our backs
Against its maddening strength
Aside we shoved its threat
Hoping it soon would cease.
It did not cease
But bathed us with
Sand and mud
Forcing trees to bow
Uprooting foundations.

It bears a new name
They call it hurricane
It confiscates our leisure
With immeasurable pleasure
Bringing strange fever
With stormy migraine
For we thought
It soon will vanish
But lo!
Our houses are
Pulverized
They call it hurricane.

Nora Omoverere Gbagi

Echoes of Hardship

It's the sigh of a mother on sighting
The depleting bag of garri.
It's the vain attempt to stretch the last tuber of yam
For fictitious months in a household of six,
when in truth, we know that it only has two days service left in it.
It's the reason mother sends the prettiest of her girls to the
    shy meat man
For yet another credit purchase.
The reason she turns partially blind and deaf when the second
    oldest comes home
with strange money in hand,
and ambiguous tales on her tongue.
It's the sound that distracts the hardworking, but strangely
    still penniless Trader
From the insults showered by his razor-tongued wife.

It's the echo of hard times,
the sound outside our doors.
shut the doors and windows!
stuff the cracks in the walls!
by all means, keep the sound at bay!
cos like the sirens song,
all who hear it must fall under its spell
and slowly, the oil will dry
gradually the jingling of coins against each other
fades and the market square empties out of not just buyers
but even the traders and their wares.

It's the echo of hard times,
The sound outside our doors.

Nnenna May George-Kalu

The Divide

We met in the school playground
Her children and mine studied together
We spotted each other across the field
For of all the parents, our skin colour was similar
There was recognition in her eyes, and mine

We met again in that playground
The children milling around in freedom
Then I saw the veil and full skirt of her religion
She observed my hair flying free and my arms bare
There was caution in her eyes, and mine

We met at the car park, mothers running late
She called out to her daughter and I to mine
I heard that name and it was Zainab
She heard me call the name and it was Ezinne
There was curiosity in her eyes, and mine

We sat next to each other at the parents meeting
The fidgety children played close by us
I am Nigerian whispered Zainab
Well, so am I stated Ezinne in surprise
There was excitement in her eyes, and mine

We met at the school play for the end of the year
The news that morning was on both our minds
Our country's president was dead and he was from her tribe
The Vice president had taken over and he was from mine tribe
There was suspicion in her eyes, and in mine

We met at their send-off to return home for good
I brought her a present but she got me one too
We unwrapped them instantly, full make-up sets both
Our tastes were similar, veiled or unveiled
There was regret in her eyes, and in mine

Folake Idowu

Away from Home

I bridge the tip of my fingers
Massaging the lancing ache
Winter they call it
It travels from my frozen lips
Wedges on my wide hips
Making me click and my steps clack
Icy slabs slick

I hold off uncertainty
My hands numb
Printed paper legitimizes me
In this cold land
Permits and certificates
To pledge identity
Once I thought I already owned

I breathe air into parched nostrils
The sharp dryness
Makes me cough
One must not be sick
Health insurance there is none
Hospital charges intolerant of poor
No credit or loans acknowledged

Within their glances suppositions rage
Stereotypes battling globalisation
Trapped in a cage marked with my name
Run away I try
Nowhere to hide
Far away from home
My future auctioned at price unknown

I pray for belonging
Till lips ache and tongue bleeds
My nomadic soul seeks new solace
Promised lands glitter over the horizon
Canada and America
Eldorados with trees dangling gold bars
Mirages for a parched brain

Reveries filled with territories soaked in colour
My spirit garbed in ankara and adire
Soaring high in *aso oke* and haze
Adorn me with cultural beauty
No explanations warranting
My people know me
As I know them

I dream of friends lost
Homeland calls without phone cards
Desperate words stumble unvoiced
Save me from myself
From this place
Where black is black and that is that
Against this daily tide I rise

My own seen but unknown
My skin
My colour
My hope
This mirrored reflection casts old shadows
So much more to me than I am
An unwelcome traveller far from home

Dinah Ishaku

The Baring Days

Till they came from the west
My people looked their best
Bare but below the waist
Now they are draped in vests
Oh what a waste!

Intruding invaders from the seas
Surely on shore what you had to see
Must have filled you with untold glee
Yet if it displeased you why not flee

Instead you ruined our beauty with sin
Sin of covering a work of masterpiece
Now with sorrow I have to agree
With what you say is deemed fit

Though multitudes must be convinced
That this veiling is chaste
I still long for the baring days
I know it would save a lot the stolen peeks!

Anthonia C. Kalu

Distribution of Wealth

He sits between us,
As we buckle-up for the Lagos flight.
I used to be a pilot
For a small distribution company:
He confides in condescending tones.
I nod, holding my smile,
As we reach cruising altitude
In the sun-washed skies
Suffused with memories
Of death-spewing machines.

You are too young
To remember
How not to eat
Bland airplane cake
With your mouth open.
Thoughts of his wealth, exploited
Fill you with current pleasures
Denying you access to simple accounting.
You try to hold his blue
With your brash brown gaze,
To demand his acquiescence
To your yearnings for more gold
He smiles, and gives you his cake.

Oh-h-h, you just missed
His darting gaze,
Across the aisle,
To the other seat he paid for
When you went to the toilet
To polish your face,
To admire the gold bangles
He bought you,
From Ghana, Cape Town or Cairo.

He already craves
The pleasures
Of her cool-brown gaze, and
The jingle-jangle of the gold bangles
He bought her,
From Abu Dhabi, India or China.
His next flight is east.
He, the new machine, he flies;
Spewing death.

Without Strife

Mocking life,
Wielding knives at bullets,
The journey home
Is studded
With the blood of hope
And memories of us
Marching to nationhood,
Without strife.

It makes sense
To fetch firewood for Mother
In forests dense with landmines
Where the danger
Promised a nation of patriots,
Stalks children brave enough to fish for sixpence
In pockets full of holes,
And snares the memories of elders
Hungry for the tart-peace of bitterleaf soup.

Born in plenty,
Yesterday's youths of valor
Gave birth to elders
Whose dormant courage
Forgets trailblazers and history;
To bury women in unmarked graves
Of homesteads lost to nations,
Without might,
Giving way to hunger, poverty and dread
In places where promised futures lurk unheeded.

It makes more sense
To birth a future of dreams
Filled with lion children
Who, fetching Life
From living embers
Of dying homesteads,
Will again stoke the souls of ancestors
Who dreamed our Homeland
As a place,
Without strife.

Naomi Lucas

Trading Places

I see me
Hair short and curly, my skin a colour I'm yet to define
Four years of weight gain capsules, my waist's still a 24
5 feet without heels, my bust's a modest 32
The first of four girls, and the smallest too

"Lepa Shandy!" they yelled as I walked past
The sound of their cruel jests, always made my knees falter
There was a time I used to cry, but now I'm all grown
"Don't take it to heart" mum always said, holding my hand
    tenderly in her own

I see you
Your hair just the opposite of mine, tied in a loose ponytail
I liked the way your skin glowed in the midday sun, clear and
    smooth, and soft, I was almost certain
The roundness of your face reminded me of the cherubs I used
    to trace, in "My Book of Bible Stories"
You filled out your clothes really nicely; I didn't think you had
    any worries

You wore slippers and still towered above me; I wondered how
    you got that lucky
"Wow!" I thought; God did take his time with you
I closed my eyes, haunted by what you had that I didn't,
wishing if only temporarily, that I could be like you
How lovely it must be to sway those hips from side to side,
and not have to worry about finding my dress size,
at the shop in Ojodu

I opened my eyes, you were looking at me
I didn't know that at that same moment
You liked my short and curly hair, and also my waistline
I didn't know the size of your boobs, had strained your back
      for so long
I didn't know they called you "Orobo" and you cried every time
      you went home

We laugh about that day now, seeing the futility of it all
But doesn't it amaze you still
That when you looked at me and I at you
We both wanted to trade places?

Kate Mshelia

Vanity

If I sleep tonight, I don't want to ever wake up
My weary eyes fatigued
Tired at looking at this sinful world
My body, so weak from day to day struggles
Struggles that lead to nowhere—but damnation
I want to go somewhere and get drunk
But I believe the world won't approve
Of a woman coming home staggering
But where else will I quench my sorrows
But in the bosom of alcohol
Yes the world will definitely be alarmed
You'll one day say you need to be responsible
Nobody will want a drunk for a wife
This is Africa
But who needs marriage
Who needs a family
Who needs to bring forth children into this world
Who needs to bring more sorrow, add more pain
Our parents were ignorant when they brought us
Or were they just plain wicked
Did they know about this sinful world
Yet they gave birth to us
Abeg* somebody help me Answer

---

* *Abeg* means please in Nigerian pidgin English.

Emmanuella Nduonofit

It's All About "Her" . . .

(1)
We were all sleeping together
but it was she they picked up from bed

The next day we saw her
raped
deeply bruised everywhere
no tongue
a hole on her head

And we never slept together again

(2)
There were strong, courageous warriors in the troubled land
but it was she who infiltrated

Her beauty held them all
and their king had her;
she gave birth,
was part of them

When she returned,
the land had trouble no more.

(3)
They were true loves everlasting
but it was she who was jilted

She saw him
sleeping with another in his arms
and her vengeance is:
dormant acid on his face
from a pipe

When he woke up,
he did not know himself

(4)
At election time
it was she who contested

When she came out
her nation in her heart
her folk in her soul
they all said, *"No!*

She is not fit.
He is."

(5)
They were both loving, caring parents
but it was she they pushed into marriage

to a man her grandfather's age,
a chief of five old wives.
He forced her to bed
and she had the clap and another

He drove her away
because she stank and burns

(6)
In a nation of weak people
it was she who sacrificed

She was with them at the forefront
when the other side gained momentum
She killed the best,
went for so many
and lastly herself

The nation drinks her blood
and gets invigorated for future fights.

Adora Neboh

Loss of Glory

The mahogany trees of my land
Have been felled
And singing birds
Taken to flight
The seams of my being
Have been undone
I am not the same person
I used to be

It is a blind spot
What my eyes used to see
There are no more tears
My rivers refuse to flow
No more dreams
Not even in black and white

I poke at the ashes
Searching for a glow
I dig up the shrub-less soil
And there are no corpses to bury
No cold and soothing hugs
From the withered arms
No kisses
From the lips of the dead

There is nothing to live for
No passion to die for
My vacant eyes stare
Unoccupied for nobody lives here
I stare at yards and yards
Of empty space
Years and years
Of nothingness

Yes I can see the future
Not for me the fortune teller's lies
Divinations end in exasperation
Agony and condemnation
But in this desolate land
Dwells a sacred dare
So I bend over and dig
And strike a notion
The magic of conception
Hope for my weary heart

Ifeyinwa Genevieve Okolo

Just a Little Cut

Just a cut, a little cut
And you are on your way to womanhood.

Nothing is said about the unsterilized blade,
The crooked needle for sewing,
The herbal putty to cover the laceration,
The funny way of walking before healing,
The infections and uncountable deaths,
Aha! And HIV is in town.

No, they said.
Infection is for girls
Scared of taking up the responsibilities of womanhood.
Death certainly is a proof
Of their unworthiness for that upward call.

And so we filed into the dark room
Like sheep to the slaughter
Sliced, diced, sewn and left to groan.
Survivors of the ordeal
Danced to the village square,
Bodies decorated with camwood.
Beautiful virtuous women, ripe for marriage at ten.

Nine months is a short time.
The baby kicks, eager to see the light.
Something is wrong: he cannot smoothly glide out.
Push, the midwife says.
The gritting and screaming pass unnoticed.
Push harder, the stern command insists.
Somehow only the owner hears the sound of tearing flesh
The gully is in place and baby's big head shows up.

Ah, it is a baby boy!
The father must be proud, and proud he is.
And the mother?
Oh, she is in seclusion
Where the stench of her ever pouring urine, faeces too,
Does not embarrass the guests.

Wedding Night

It is my wedding night.
He hovers outside my door
Just long enough to knock and clear his throat—
His best and only foreplay.

Huge and hard
Heavy breathing his musical accompaniment
He demands entry
But heaven's gate is locked:
I have been sewn up.

Heaven's gate has a tiny peephole
Labeled: Fluids Only—
5 minutes for my champagne
10 days for my red wine
And my husband struggles on the other side.

Patience is not the plea for this moment.
It stands helpless:
My husband alone it endures
But, he is armed with an antelope's horn
Designed just for this purpose over ages.
With the horn he pierces.
My peephole now gapes:
Heaven's gate at last has a key!

He barges in
Unmindful of my screams,
The tear and my tears,
The blood—my blood, red as wine.
One more time, he has proven himself a man
And I, I have become a woman.

H. Obiageli Okolocha

Prisoners, Us

Gloomy eyes peeping out of the Black Maria driving past
For goodness sake—who gave this vehicle such a name?
Maria—Sacrilege!
This sacrilege to convey Prisoners?
THINK! Prisoners . . . they?
Psssh, aren't we all Prisoners?
In the prison and constraints of life, the prison of conscience
Imprisoned by religion, by insecurities?
In the prison of our humanity, the prison of desires
Imprisoned by marriage, by love?
In the prison of our traditions, the prison of culture
Imprisoned by illnesses, by egos, attitudes?
Yes, we ride in the Black Maria with gloomy eyes
All of us, Prisoners!

Ify Omalicha

You Came at Sunrise

You came at sunrise

bearing the message of love

My door parted in two at your presence

By noon
>   your silence filled my room . . .

My spirit scarred
>   with the burns of your touch . . .

You followed the night
>   and never returned . . .

Yewande Omotoso

The Trains

Yesterday the trains made me cry.

Not the woman with fat fingers
who left nuts on the floor.
Not the three girls who sat together
heads bent over a soiled magazine.

Not the old woman with gums for teeth
a garbage bag of her valuables
left in the middle of the aisle
while she nodded off on the end row.
I worried she'd miss her stop
but was too afraid to wake her.

Yesterday's trains made me cry.

Not because people entered brazen
then when security came
they had a clever story
for why first class got confused for third.

The trains were full yesterday.

Carriages of workers moving home,
gorged and disgorged at each station.
People squashed but looked away, no contact.
They stood frozen, age on their faces.

The trains were full yesterday
then a little girl got on
her face wrapped in bandages
a bright pink bag on her back.
Everyone turned,
the three girls, the old woman, me.

"How are you?" I asked. "What's your name?"
She talked easy with a big voice,
And my eyes stung to see her
emboldened by what life had brought.

I reached through the space between strangers
to the silent weary mother
"Your daughter is lovely," I said.
She nodded agreement but smiled
something sad I couldn't have known.

"Our turn Mommy." The doors slid open.
The little girl held her mother's hand and pulled.
"She is beautiful," the mother said to me
"Even with the burns, she's beautiful."

The girl stayed with me.
Somedays I call on her courage,
conjure up the fierce look she wore.
It has since become my prayer
to greet whatever the day
with her same spunk, her lightness.

Olajumoke Verissimo

Divorcee

we parted
we met
we parted
we met
we parted
we met
we melted
as memories.

Appendix:
Poems as Written in
Their Original Languages

Edna Merey Apinda

Le secret de la nuit

Dites au vent
De porter ces paroles
Vers celui pour qui
Mon cœur bât

Dites à la rivière
De porter mes pas
Vers celui
Qui m'attend.

Dites au temps
De s'arrêter
Quand il posera
Sur moi son regard.

Dites à la nuit
D'être très discrète
Qu'elle garde pour elle
Le secret de nos lèvres.

Dites au jour
De retarder sa venue
Que nos mains encore
Restent enlacées.

Peu importe

Je chante, je danse, je ris
Je vis comme si demain n'existait pas
Je mens comme si personne ne m'écoutait
La vie m'entraine comme une douce mélodie
J'avance sans me soucier de l'avenir

Mais parfois
Quand la nuit est tombée et que personne n'écoute
Je dis des prières en secret
Pour que demain soit clair
Plein de promesses

Car souvent
La vie est triste de ce côté-ci de la planète
Elle se montre cruelle
Laisse orphelins, affamés ou fous.
Et ils courent
Vers plus de richesse en vendant âme au diable
En oubliant celui qui vit haut dans le ciel

Je chante, je danse
Je ris, je vis
Comme si demain se fera plus doux
Je rêve qu'il soit plus simple comme
Les jours d'avant.

Car trop souvent
Ils avancent comme des bêtes de somme
Bercés par des prêches d'un genre nouveau
Qui regarde au fond du porte-monnaie
Afin de conduire les âmes à Dieu.

On croit se jouer de la vie
Qui nous fait laid ou pauvre
On en veut toujours plus
Et pourquoi?
On craint demain, l'autre, son prochain
On se croit supérieur à tout.

Or nous ne sommes que des humains
Et demain
Nous trouvera tels quels
Mendiants en quête d'amour
Croyants espérant le salut
Miséreux ayant un cœur en or
Hommes.

Je chante sur un air tendre
Je ris des faux prophètes nouveaux roi en ce pays
Je pleure face à l'humain qui se perd
Face à la quête de l'argent à tout prix
Les valeurs se perdent et j'espère

Demain qui sera mieux
Qui chantera
Qui nous fera danser.

Harriet Naboro

Leave Me Alone

Cer… cer	[Luo]
Ih ongoba nga cere?	[Samia]
Twazala bano abana	[Luganda]
Mumukwano nga twagalana	[Luganda]
Cha cha cha	[Samia]
Sisidaha	[Samia]
Naye jukira je twwayitamu	[Luganda]
Kati ongoba ngende bwomu?	[Luganda]
You are such a fool	[English]
Iming iming ful	[Luo]
Let us talk, what do you think?	[English]
I don't want; sitaki takataka	[English/Swahili]
Eh won latin	[Luo]
Eh cer tin	[Luo]
I don't want you in my house	[English]
Kale mwami nkangende ewa Silausi	[Luganda]

Nathalie Hoblebou Ouandaogo/Rouamba

Hommage aux Enfants Soldats

Pourquoi ne vois-je pas le jour?
Pourquoi ne vois-je pas le bout du tunnel?
Pourquoi cette nuit interminable?
Ces bruits qui sifflent dans mes oreilles.
Mon cœur qui ne reconnait plus la lumière.
Mon cœur qui rejette la justice.
Ce cœur qui méprise la vérité.
Ce cœur qui refuse de battre.
Est-il mien?

Poeme: Amertum

Ce sentiment de culpabilité qui me tient au cou et ne me lâche pas.
Qu'ai-je fait? Peut-on ainsi se tromper? Demander pardon? Suis-je
vraiment coupable? Qui d'ailleurs à tort? Question difficile
à répondre quand on se la pose.

La survie, cet instinct qui nous pousse souvent à l'extrême, avec
comme seul but sauver sa peau au prix du mensonge,
 de la trahison et
de fois même du meurtre.
J'accuse: l'homme; la société, réel
bourreau, juge subjectif qui engendre ses
calamités.

Ami! Je te cherche. Dans tes yeux j'avais découvert un monde
merveilleux. J'ai beau fouiller, l'horizon reste vide de toi. Etais-tu un
mirage? Tu semblais si réel, unique dans
cette obscurité.

Thérèse Kuoh-Moukoury

Le trône perdu

Loin est le temps
Où j'étais assise sur tes genoux
Ta poitrine, dossier bien aimé
Portait le poids de mes jeunes années
Sous mes yeux le maïs tournait en pâte
Par l'effort de tes bras
Mes plus sûrs accoudoirs
En vain je cherche par le monde
La chaleur de ce trône perdu
En vain, la douceur de ton dos
premier univers entouré de mes bras
En vain, l'image de ces marigots
Où, pour les enfants d'Afrique
Tu te faisais lavandière
Tu chantais joyeuse, parmi d'autres déesses des ombres
Une mangue sauvage entrainait dans sa chute
Un sourd fracas et une nuée d'enfants
J'accourais, tu secouais la tête
Tout est fini, je le sais
Mais je garde à jamais
Les marques de tes seins sur ma poitrine

Danse

J'ai mis ma robe de cauris
Avance homme noir
Homme au masque de fer
Homme au masque de bois
Vois ma peau d'ébène parée de raphias
Regarde, admire, les perles
Miroiter aux cous de tes femmes
Je suis l'élue du jour
La promesse des dieux
Mon coeur plein de désir guette la nuit mystérieuse
Du pagne ancestal, me voici revêtue
Dansons le Yabo rituel, échangeons nos flammes
Mes jambes de gazelle se profilent entre les nattes murales
Et ton ombre légère glisse entre les lucioles
Dansons le Yabo, la danse divine de nos pères
Dansons le Yabo, dansons
Bientôt le chant du coq va mettre fin à notre danse

l'Art d'Afrique

Afrique
J'aime ta musique
        ta sculpture
        ta peinture
Je me reconnais
en ces héroïnes de ton passé
Je ressemble à ces femmes
de tes gravures rupestres
fussent-elles de la forêt du Congo
        des steppes du Sahel
        des monts d'Adamaoua
        du Lac Tanganyika,
Je leur ressemble!
Mon âme gravée sur leur visage
Rappelle les temps dorés
Où mon coeur aimait et souffrait

J'aime ta sculpture
Tes statues de bois, de terre, d'ivoire, d'or
ont fixé à jamais l'humain dans la magie
de la beauté
 la jouissance
 la puissance
aux confins de l'éternité

J'aime ta musique
Pareille à la naissance du monde
Elle seule, complice du temps
dit les souffrances de nos coeurs
dans un langage plus riche que les mots
Chaleur, Soleil, Lumière
Ô tam-tam tam! tam-tam tam!
Ô musique
suspendue sur les cordes du mvet
aux sons des trompettes
sur les doigts du flûtiste
aux voix divines des sirènes, des déesses et des anges
Art d'Afrique, art d'Afrique, ton chant: un éternel poème

Biographical Notes

Imali Abala (b. 1962) is associate professor in the Department of English at Ohio Dominican University. She is author of three novels: *The Dilemma of Jahenda the Teenage Mother* (2010), *The Disinherited* (2007), and *Move on, Trufosa* (2006).

Monica D. Aciru (b. 1980) is from Kampala, Uganda. She currently resides in Belgium and is working on a PhD in criminology at Catholic University in Leuven. She also holds a BA in social sciences and an MA in peace and conflict studies from Makerere University, and a master of governance and development studies from the University of Antwerp.

Toyin Adewale-Gabriel (b. 1969) is a fellow of the Akademie Schloss Solitude and previously has been writer in residence at the Villa Waldberta, Munich, and the Baltic Centre for Writers and Translators, Visby, Sweden. In 2001, her poem "Shelter of Rain" won third prize at the Musical Society of Nigeria Poetry Awards. During 1998–1999, she was editor of the *ANA Review*, official journal of the Association of Nigerian Authors. In 1991, she founded Women Writers of Nigeria. Her publications include *Naked Testimonies* (1995, 2006), *Die Aromaforscherin* (1998), and *Bitter Chocolate* (2010).

Oghomwensemwen "Oghomwen" Aimie Adeyinka-Edward (b. 1983) studied at Dalhousie University and the Toronto Film School. She has written for both Nigerian and international publications such as *Wedding Planner* and *Amoi* magazines, and writes scripts for television and film.

Akachi Adimora-Ezeigbo (b. 1947) is professor of English at the University of Lagos. From 1997 to 2000 she was vice president of the Women Writers' Association of Nigeria, and from 2002 to 2011 she was vice president of PEN Nigeria. She is a novelist, short story writer, playwright, and children's author, and has won six major literary prizes. Her five novels include the award-winning *House of Symbols* (2001) and *Roses and Bullets* (2011), based on the events of the Nigerian/Biafran War. Her poetry collection, *Heart Songs,* won the ANA/Cadbury Poetry Prize in 2009. She has also published more than twenty children's books.

Omofolabo Ajayi-Soyinka (b. 1950) was born, raised, and educated in Nigeria, but now lives in the United States. She is professor of theater and women, gender, and sexuality studies at the University of Kansas. Her teaching and research focus on critical analysis of gender aesthetics in the literary and performing arts and cultural paradigms in Africa and the diaspora. She is author of numerous publications and is currently working on the plays of Efua Sutherland, and a book of poems.

Umma Aliyu Musa (b. 1976) is Hausa language lecturer at the Universität Hamburg and is pursuing her PhD at the Universität Leipzig in Germany. She is a member of the Association of Nigerian Authors, and was a copresenter of the radio program "Poetic Minds" at Radio Kano. She has also worked at the American University of Nigeria as associate director and acting director of admission. Her poetry has been published in the *Weekly Trust* newspaper.

Epifania Akosua Amoo-Adare was born in London in 1967. She has dual British and Ghanaian citizenship. She is a social science researcher and educator with more than twenty-six years of experience working in diverse locations such as Afghanistan, Armenia, Azerbaijan, Georgia, Ghana, Qatar, the United Kingdom, and the United States. She also works with Reach Out to Asia of the Qatar Foundation, where she conducts research in support of the organization's mission to provide access to quality basic education, to engage youth as leaders, and to conduct advocacy on youth development within the Middle East and Asia.

Edna Merey Apinda was born in Libreville, Gabon, in 1976, and currently lives and works in Port-Gentil. Apinda is one of the most active young writers of Gabon. She regularly visits schools across Gabon to promote literature and reading, and recently accepted an invitation to the United States to present lectures on her creative works. In addition to writing short stories and poetry, she is also the author of five books: *Les aventures d'Imya, petite fille du Gabon* (2004), *Ce soir, je fermerai la porte* (2006), *Garde le sourire* (2008), *Des contes pour la lune* (2010), and *Ce reflet dans le miroir* (2011).

Arecau is the pen name of Philippa Ndisi-Herman. Ndisi-Herman lives in Nairobi.

Joyce Ashuntantang is assistant professor of English at the University of Hartford and associate to the UNESCO chair and Institute for Comparative Human Rights at the University of Connecticut. She is also founder of EduART Inc., a nonprofit organization created to promote art as a medium for social change. An actress, poet, screenwriter, and filmmaker, she is the author of several books including *Landscaping Postcoloniality: The Dissemination of Anglophone Cameroon Literature* (2009), and a poetry collection, *A Basket of Flaming Ashes* (2010).

Temitope Azeez-Stephen (b. 1983) is a human resource consultant for H. Pierson Associates in Lagos Island, Nigeria. She is working on her MA in business administration at Heriot-Watt University, Edinburgh Business School.

Unoma Azuah (b. 1969) teaches English at Lane College in Jackson, Tennessee. She is a multiple award-winning writer, winning the Hellman/Hammett award, the Urban Spectrum award, the Nwapa/NDDC award, and the Leonard Trawick award. She also won the Aidoo-Snyder Book award for her most recent novel, *Edible Bones*.

T. Mojisola Bakare (b. 1961) has a degree in business administration, but her love for the spoken word and English literature brought her back to the arts in late 2009. She is currently working on a stage play project, a film, and her own collection of poems.

Damilola Balogun (b. 1986) was born and raised in Nigeria, where she currently resides and is pursuing a career in graphic design.

Bonita Belle (b. 1982) is the pen name of Cynthia Ogana. Her poems appear in *Counterpoint and Other Poems*.

Nadia Z. Bishai (b. 1937) is professor emeritus of English at the University of Alexandria. Her main field of research is the relationship between poetry and music. She studied piano at the Alexandria Conservatory of Music and in London with concert pianists Ilona Kabos and Denis Matthews, and has performed at the Opera House in Alexandria.

Nana Nyarko Boateng (b. 1986) lives in Accra and works as a writer and broadcast journalist with Citi FM and *The Globe*. She has a BA in English and political science from the University of Ghana.

Rose Wanjiru Busolo (née Mukuria) was born in Kenya in 1969, and now lives in British Columbia, Canada. In 1994, her poems were featured in *Presense,* a local magazine in Nairobi, and she has been writing ever since.

Cheshe Dow is from Gaborone, Botswana, and holds a juris doctor degree from the University of Cincinnati, College of Law. She currently works in the financial services sector in the area of legal and compliance risk management. She is a contributor to *African Women Writing Resistance: An Anthology of Contemporary Voices.*

Love Chioma Enwerem is on the staff of Imo State University, Nigeria. She is a member of the Association of Nigerian Authors. She is an advocate for gender justice and equity, and has presented papers on the subject at a number of international conferences. She is author of the poetry anthology, *As the Sun Rises*, and has published a number of short stories and plays in journals. She is currently working on her second anthology of poems and a collection of short stories.

Lydia E. Epangué (b. 1987) is studying for an MA in contemporary media at the University of Wolverhampton in England, and is currently working on her first novel.

Nora Omoverere Gbagi (b. 1984) is a human resource manager with a telecommunication infrastructure provider in Lagos, Nigeria.

Nnenna May George-Kalu (b. 1974) is a lawyer by training and has practiced as a barrister and solicitor in both private and public law in her home country, Nigeria. In a voluntary capacity, she has been involved in projects targeting reproductive health and rights of women and adolescents in her community. Her voluntary work led her to be selected for a MacArthur Foundation fellowship coordinated by Pathfinder International. She is author of *Hate Your Neighbour as Yourself*, published as part of a project to combat campus cultism in Nigeria, and continues to employ creative and academic writing as a medium of social change. She currently lives in Birmingham, England.

Nicole Elisha Hartzenberg (b. 1992) is a medical student at the University of Stellenbosch.

Folake Idowu was born in Lagos, Nigeria, but left to study in England during her teens. An avid writer of children's fiction, she has been nominated for three awards, including Macmillan's Write for Africa competition. Her short stories for adults have been published in various anthologies such as *AWP* (2009), *Onwards* (2010), and *Offshoots* (2011). She currently lives in Geneva, Switzerland.

Dinah Ishaku (b. 1982) is a litigation attorney and member of several writing forums in Abuja, Nigeria. She studied law at the University of Maiduguri and got called to the Nigerian Bar as an attorney and solicitor of the Supreme Court of Nigeria in 2009.

Isabella Jeso (née Isabella Pupurai Matsikidze) is lecturer in the Department of English at the University of Vermont. She is author of both creative and scholarly works, including the collection of poems, *The Zimbabwean Collectibles*. She is currently working on another book of poems, *Memorials of Our Redemption: A Woman Epic of Zimbabwe*.

Anthonia C. Kalu is professor of African American and African studies at Ohio State University and previously taught at the University of Northern Colorado. Kalu is an active member of the African Studies Association and the African Literature Association and is the current president of the African Literature Association. Her publications include *Women, Literature and Development in Africa* (2001), *Broken Lives and Other Stories* (2003), and the *Rienner Anthology of African Literature* (2007), which won *ForeWord* Magazine's Book of the Year Award in 2007.

Njeri Kang'ethe (b. 1955) is a gender and human rights consultant in Nairobi. A prolific writer and social commentator who has published in Kenya and elsewhere, Njeri is passionate about social justice. She is an advocate of the High Court of Kenya and a certified international investigator for gross violations of human rights and humanitarian law and the coordinator of the Senior Clergy Consultative Forum (SCCF), a fellowship of retired heads of churches and denominations that supports and advises the church leadership in matters of justice, peace, healing, and reconciliation. She was a 2010/11 Fulbright scholar-in-residence and adjunct faculty member in the Gender and Women's Studies Department of the State University of New York, Plattsburgh.

Susan Nalugwa Kiguli (b. 1969) is senior lecturer and department chair in the Department of Literature at Makerere University and has served as the chairperson of the Uganda Women Writers' Association. She held the 2010–2011 American Council of Learned Societies/African Humanities Fellowship, and is a 2011 African Studies Association Presidential Fellow.

Thérèse Kuoh-Moukoury (b. 1938) studied in her native Cameroon until the age of 12, and then continued her education in France. She is a docteur-ès-lettres with a specialization in law and education. She is considered one of the pioneers of African feminism postindependence, and has worked in journalism, media, and publishing. Her novel, *Rencontres essentielles* (1969), is a classic of African women's writing and has been translated into English as *Essential Encounters* (2002).

Naomi Lucas is a Nigerian writer, social commentator, and brand strategist. She heads the Business Development and Brand Management unit of the Africa Movie Academy Awards. She recently attended the Farafina Trust Creative Writing Workshop hosted by Chimamanda Adichie. She is currently working on her first novel and a collection of short stories.

Makuchi, the pen name of Juliana Nfah-Abbenyi, is a literary critic and writer, and professor of English and comparative literature at North Carolina State University. Her publications include *Gender in African Women's Writing: Identity, Sexuality, and Difference, Your Madness, Not Mine: Stories of Cameroon,* and *The Sacred Door and Other Stories: Cameroon Folktales of the Beba.*

Serah Mbatia (b. 1977) is a writer with a diploma in creative writing from the Writers Bureau. She has published both nonfiction and fiction in print and online magazines.

Frida Menkan Mbunda-Nekang (b. 1970) is head of the Department of English at the University of Buea, Cameroon. She has also studied at the University of Yaoundé, the University of Nigeria, and Kogi State University in Nigeria. She is author of *Wonder Tales from Oku, Aesthetics of Storytelling,* and *Shadows from the Abyss,* a collection of poems.

Cheseche S. Mibenge was born in Zambia. She currently lives in New York and teaches human rights at Lehman College. Her publications include *Show Me a Woman! Narratives of Gender and Violence in Human Rights.*

Kate Mshelia has a BA in English from the University of Maiduguri.

Lenah Mukoya (b. 1986) is an undergraduate student in architecture at Jomo Kenyatta University of Agriculture and Technology in Kenya.

Sandra Mushi (b. 1974) is an interior architecture designer with a passion for writing. She was born in Dar es Salaam, grew up in the United Kingdom, and was educated in Tanzania, Botswana, and South Africa. She is the author of *The Rhythm of My Rhyme*, a collection of soulful poems that address the choices, challenges, and consequences of women's and children's rights.

Bernedette Muthien is cofounder and director of Engender, a nongovernmental organization that works in the areas of gender and sexuality, human rights, and peace and justice. Her community activism is integrally related to her work with continental and international organizations and her research reflects the values of equity, societal transformation, and justice. She coconvenes the Global Political Economy Commission of the International Peace Research Association, is a member of Amanitare, the African network of gender activists, and Africa editor of the international journal *Queries*. She is cofounder of an indigenous scholar-activist network, the KhoeSan Women's Circle, and convenor of an international listserv of Native scholar-activists, Gender Egalitarian.

Rosalyn Mutia (b. 1966) is senior lecturer at the University of Yaoundé, where she teaches American and Commonwealth literature. Her main areas of specialization are gender and feminist studies, and she has published several scholarly articles in local and international journals on those subjects. A former German Academic Exchange Service scholar at the University of Bayreuth, she also has been adjunct professor at Dickinson College in Pennsylvania.

Connie Mutua (b. 1988) writes and blogs about human experiences, focusing on discrimination and oppression. Her poetry appears in the anthology *African Sexualities* (edited by Sylvia Tamale).

Harriet Naboro (b. 1979) earned a BA in literature and drama from Makerere University and has published poems in several anthologies.

Monica Mweliya Nambelela was born in a refugee camp of Lubango in Angola during Namibia's bitter fight for freedom. She grew up in Germany and mostly writes in German. She has published two poems in the German-Namibian literature magazine, *Felsgrafiti,* and is currently working on a book (in German) with five other Namibian women on issues pertaining to the situation of women in Africa.

Sitawa Namwalie is the pen name of Betty Muragori. She is a Kenyan poet, writer, and performer who is interested in how contemporary Africans define themselves. She works as a development consultant in the areas of environment, gender, and governance. Her first performed poetry show, *Cut off My Tongue*, met with huge success in Nairobi in 2008 and was published in 2009. Nominated for the 2010 Freedom to Create Prize, she is currently touring Kenya and Uganda with her second dramatized poetry, *Homecoming*, to rave reviews.

Emmanuella Nduonofit (b. 1977) has a BA in English from Nnamdi Azikiwe University in Nigeria.

Adora Neboh (b. 1978) is a human resources professional in Lagos. She studied theater arts at the University of Nigeria, Nsukka. She posts her poems on a poetry blog.

Mercy Ngigi (b. 1990) is a writer and artist in Thika, central

Kenya. She is studying mass communication and psychology at Daystar University in Nairobi, where she is editor in chief of the *Daystar Portal* and also tutor at the university's Writing and Speech Centre.

Patience Nitumwesiga is a member of the Uganda Women Writers' Association.

Wandia Njoya is a poet, blogger, and university lecturer in Kenya. She grew up in Kenya and spent a number of years in the United States, where she earned a degree in African literature in French at Pennsylvania State University.

Pat T. Nkweteyim (b. 1968) teaches theater arts at the University of Buea, and is head of the Multimedia Resource Centre of Government Bilingual High School in Limbe. She is currently working on a PhD in media studies at the University of Calabar in Nigeria.

Beverley Nambozo Nsengiyunva (b. 1976) is a Ugandan writer and poet, and founder of the annual poetry award for Ugandan women called the BN Poetry Award, which began in 2008. Currently she is working on her MA in creative writing from Lancaster University in the United Kingdom. In November 2011, she was selected to represent female poets of East Africa at the second African Women Writers' Symposium in Johannesburg, South Africa, which coincided with the celebration of Nadine Gordimer's eighty-eighth birthday. She is currently working on her second collection of poetry and her first novel.

Jasmine Ntoutoume was born in Japan to a Jamaican mother and a Gabonese father. She is a freelance music journalist who lives and works in Freiburg, Germany. After spending her formative years in Jamaica, she moved to Canada where she studied French literature and art history. She published her first poem at age seven in Jamaica and continues to write poetry today.

Jemeo Nyonjo (b. 1976) is a volunteer with the African Writers' Trust and a member of the Uganda Women Writers' Association.

Her poems have been published in *New Era* magazine, *Wordwrite Literary Journal*, *The Torture Watch* (a biannual newsletter of the African Centre for Treatment and Rehabilitation of Torture Victims), and *Michael's Eyes—The War Against the Ugandan Child* (edited by Raoul J. Granqvist). Nyonjo also writes in Luganda, her mother tongue, and has a number of poems and short stories published in the Lugandan magazine *Entanda ya Buganda*.

Jennifer A. Okech (b. 1985) writes poetry, short stories, and scripts for screen and radio. She is associate editor of the *Daily Monitor*, one of Uganda's main English dailies, and is a member the Uganda Women Writers' Association. Her publications have appeared in the anthologies *Talking Tales* (Violet Barungi, ed.) and *The Butterfly Dance* (Okaka Dokatum and Rose Rwakasisi, eds.).

Ifeyinwa Genevieve Okolo (b. 1980) is a PhD student in the Department of English and a tutorial assistant with the general studies program at the University of Ibadan. Her research interests include gender and sexuality discourses in African literature.

H. Obiageli Okolocha (b. 1965) is lecturer in the Department of English and Literature at the University of Benin in Nigeria. She is interested in exploring issues of gender, feminism, and human rights in drama. She has published widely in local and international scholarly journals, and is currently expanding her academic strengths to include short stories and poetry.

Marjorie Oludhe-Macgoye (née King) was born in Southampton, England, in 1928. After studying English literature at the University of London, she worked as a bookseller and, in 1954, went to Nairobi as an employee of the Church Missionary Society Bookshop. She married D. G. W. Oludhe-Macgoye in 1960 and took Kenyan citizenship in 1964. She now lives in Nairobi. She won the Sinclair Prize for Fiction (UK) in 1986 for her novel *Coming to Birth* and the Jomo Kenyatta Literary Prize (2007) for *A Farm Called Kishinev*.

Ify Omalicha (b. 1977), one of Nigeria's youngest poets, was killed in an automobile accident on March 16, 2012. She was also an actress and performance artist, and was a fellow in the Department of Theatre Arts at the University of Ibadan. Three collections of her poetry have been published: *Amidst the Blowing Tempest, They Run Still,* and *Now that Dreams Are Born.*

Yewande Omotoso was born in Barbados in 1980 and grew up in Nigeria with her Nigerian father, West Indian mother, and two older brothers. She and her family moved to South Africa in 1992 and have lived there ever since. She is an architect; space and buildings being of interest to her second only to words and literature. Her debut novel, *Bom Boy,* was published in September 2011.

Sarah Navalayo Osembo (b. 1985) is an internal controls and risk management consultant by profession, but also an avid reader and writer. Much of her work is unpublished.

Nathalie Hoblebou Ouandaogo/Rouamba (b. 1977) holds an MA in French from West Virginia University and an MA in anthropology and rural sociology from the University of Ouagadougou. She lives in Morgantown, West Virginia.

Hilda Twongyeirwe Rutagonya is an author, poet, and editor. She is recipient of the Certificate of Recognition from the National Book Trust of Uganda for her book *Fina the Dancer.* She is a founder and member of the Uganda Women Writers' Association, where she currently works as coordinator. She lives in Kampala, Uganda.

Clara C. Swai (b. 1967) is an executive administrative secretary in Tanzania. In 2004–2008 she served as social secretary to the South African High Commission.

Mimi Harriet Uwineza (b. 1982) was born in Rwanda and currently lives in Uganda. She is studying for her master's degree in peace and conflict studies at Makerere University, and is an editor with Fountain Publishers. A human rights activist, she works at the Al Khatim Adlan Center for Enlightenment and Human Development Sudan (KACE Sudan), and previously with the Strategic Initiative for Women in the Horn of Africa (SIHA Network). She is a member of the Uganda Women Writers' Association.

Olajumoke Verissimo (b. 1979) is the author of *I Am Memory*, which in 2009 won the Carlos Idzia Ahmad Prize for a first book of poetry, won second in the Anthony Agbo Prize for Poetry, and won an honourable mention in the Association of Nigeria Prize for Poetry. Her poems have been translated and published in Macedonian, Japanese, French, Chinese, and Arabic. She participates at poetry festivals nationally and internationally and is currently working on another collection of poems.

Makhosazana Xaba has published two collections of poetry: *These Hands* (2005) and *Tongues of Their Mothers* (2008). Her poetry has been translated into Italian and Mandarin and has appeared in numerous anthologies. She also writes short stories and essays, which have also been anthologized. She is currently writing a biography about Helen Nontando (Noni) Jabavu.

Lamia Ben Youssef Zayzafoon (b. 1966), a Tunisian academic living in the United States, is assistant professor of foreign languages and literatures at the University of Alabama at Birmingham. Her areas of specialization are postcoloniality, feminist theory, and African literature, with specific emphasis on the Maghreb. She is author of *Production of the Muslim Woman: Negotiating Text, History and Ideology* (2005) and "Anne Frank Goes East: The Algerian Civil War and the Nausea of Postcoloniality" in *Balconies of the North Sea* (edited by Waciny Laredj; 2010).

Author Index

About the Book

This anthology of never-before-published poems showcases a new generation of African women poets, some familiar, some just beginning their literary careers. Their rich voices belie popular stereotypes, reflecting the diversity and dynamism of their environment. As they range across topics encompassing family and personal relationships, politics, war, and the ravages of famine and disease, they show the breadth of African women's experiences and of their thinking about issues both on the continent and globally.

Anthonia C. Kalu is professor of African American and African Studies at Ohio State University. Her numerous publications on African literature include *Women, Literature and Development in Africa* and the edited *Rienner Anthology of African Literature*, and she is also author of *Broken Lives and Other Stories*, a collection of short stories. **Juliana Makuchi Nfah-Abbenyi** is professor of English and comparative literature at North Carolina State University. She has published a collection of short stories, *Your Madness, Not Mine: Stories of Cameroon*, as well as *The Sacred Door and Other Stories: Cameroon Folktales of the Beba* and *Gender in African Womens' Writing: Identity, Sexuality, and Difference*. **Omofolabo Ajayi-Soyinka** is professor in the Departments of Theatre and Women, Gender, and Sexuality Studies at the University of Kansas. She is coeditor of *African Literature at the Millennium* and author of *Yoruba Dance: The Semiotics of Movement and Body Attitude in a Nigerian Culture*.